Retire by Design

Why a passive approach will miss the mark

RETIRE

BY

DESIGN

Why a Passive Approach Will Miss the Mark

Brandon Steele, CFP®

Contents

Disclosures

This material has been provided for general informational purposes only and does not constitute either tax or legal advice. Although we go to great lengths to make sure our information is accurate and useful, we recommend you consult a tax preparer, professional tax advisor, or lawyer.

Brandon Steele uses the DBA Mainsail Financial Group. Mainsail Financial Group is located at 11245 SE 6th Street, Suite 230, Bellevue, WA 98004 and can be reached at 425-502-7693. All securities and advisory services are offered through Commonwealth Financial Network®, Member FINRA/SIPC, a Registered Investment Adviser.

*The client stories included in this book are for illustrative purposes only and do not constitute a recommendation as to the suitability of any investment or strategy for any person or persons having circumstances similar to those portrayed, and a financial advisor should be consulted regarding your specific situation. Actual performance and results will vary.

**This book is for informational purposes. Talk to your financial advisor before making any investing decisions. Investments are subject to risk, including the loss of principal. Because investment return and principal fluctuate, shares may be worth more or less than their original value. Asset allocation and diversification do not assure a profit or protect against loss in declining markets. Some investments are not suitable for all investors, and there is no guarantee that any investing goal will be met. Past performance is no guarantee of future results.

Investing in alternative investments may not be suitable for all investors and involves special risks, such as risk associated with leveraging the investment, adverse market forces, regulatory changes, and illiquidity. There is no assurance that the investment objective will be attained.

All indices are unmanaged and investors cannot invest directly into an index. Unlike investments, indices do not incur management fees, charges, or expenses. Past performance does not guarantee future results.

The formula used for the Rule of 72 approximates the time it will take for a given amount of money to double at a given compound interest rate. Compound illustrations are not predictions of investment performance, and investment principal and interest are not guaranteed and are subject to market fluctuation.

All examples are hypothetical and for illustrative purposes only. No specific investments were used in any examples

4

Foreword

re·tire·ment | \ ri-ˈtī(-ə)r-mənt \
1a: an act of retiring; the state of being retired
b: withdrawal from one's position or occupation or from active working life
c: the age at which one normally retires, as in 'reaches retirement in May'

At least this is the way the Webster's dictionary defines it but what does it mean, really? There was a time when retirement was the part of the natural order of our lifespan. We went to school to learn a couple of things, we found an employer that is willing to hire us to do a job, and then our employer would retire us at some point later in life and we stopped working. In that timeline, if you were fortunate, your employer might even pay you for the rest of your life from a pension plan, as well. I don't want to ruin the surprise, but for most people that sequence is just not the way that it's done anymore.

In fact, the word retirement is beginning to lose a little of its shine. Below is an interesting chart about how frequently the word "retirement" is researched and its overall usage in published material over time. Interesting to note is the decline as more and more companies have ceased their pension plans and retirement savings overall have decreased.

*Chart taken from Google Books Ngram Viewer

I have been in the world of financial planning for almost 20 years and can attest to this graph. The word just doesn't mean the same as it used to. It seems like more and more, when the word comes up, it is 'sentence adjacent' to phrases like "I'll never be able to....", "Not for me, I love working...", "I have no idea if I ever could...". The bottom line is that the concept of a clear-cut retirement has changed.

However, I would put this idea forward: With all of the different ideas and emotions this term brings up, I would suggest that retirement now means more of a new chapter beginning, rather than the end of one's productive years. I have met people that are excited to retire for a (growing) number of reasons. Some want to spend more time with family, others desire the ability to do the type of work they have always *wanted* to do versus <u>had</u> to do, even a few that are now able to dive into that start-up they have always had in mind, and the list goes on and on. It has been so interesting and humbling to hear about what people want for the next chapter of their life.

No matter what the desire or goal, no matter what the timeline or duration, all of those great ideas and fabulous plans always seem to be whittled down to one key question. Can you guess? That's right. The question is, "Can we afford it?" This idea is the grand permission slip that allows the chapter change to occur.

And this, fellow readers, is where Brandon's book can help. If you want to have your permission slip signed, you need to plan. This is why Brandon and I both believe that financial planning is so critically important for everyone no matter what your personal circumstances are.

Some believe that planning is only 'for those with money'. Not true. Others feel that planning is only important later in life, also not true. Proper financial planning evolves and changes over time, but never becomes completely unnecessary, and definitely requires more than just a passive approach. This book contains all sorts of useful, practical information about the tools of planning related specifically to the chapter change called retirement. Additionally, this text is meant to provide a resource that, when combined with the given tools, can help to create your blueprint to build the retirement that you want, however you wish to define it.

Happy Planning!!

Adam Laibson, CFP®, ChSNC

About the Author

I want to thank you right out of the gate for taking the time to invest in your financial future through this reading. I am a financial advisor/CFP® professional and have been waiting to create a vehicle that helps with realistic financial planning. The old approach to general financial advice stating a simple formula that applies to everyone no longer works. Most are looking for a more thoughtful approach to this crucial topic of personal finance.

I understand the idea of simplifying things to make it easier, but the truth is, financial planning *is* complicated, and it does take some work to understand these strategies. But, with the proper tools, like this guide, and mindset, you can gain so much more control over your future. The payoff is priceless.

I grew up in a very middle-class family. I was never what I would consider broke; we had a home, we had food (although sometimes mac n cheese and pork and beans!), but we never had freedom. My family was constantly worried about the day-to-day, and finances were something we didn't address.

The challenge was, I didn't understand how things could be or what I could do to fix my situation. Nearly every aspect we will discuss in this guide, I experienced through a negative lens growing up. This contributed to a huge curiosity from an early age to learn the financial game and understand why things were the way they were, and what could be done differently.

When I was in high school, I experienced first-hand how painful a poor economic decision can be. I, like any other 16-year-old, felt I had to have a nice car. I extended myself and bought a Dodge Durango right before leaving for college. Well, when I went to college, it was a bit harder to work as much, and I very quickly ran into difficulty making payments. I had to sell the car back and was eventually tracked down after some time due to the missed payments. This was it for me; I knew I needed to figure out this financial game and it became a driving force in helping people make wise financial decisions before they have to learn the hard way.

After graduating from Washington State University (Go Cougs!) with an economics degree, I knew I had a good financial foundation. Still, I didn't have the practical experience to apply any of my knowledge. When I first learned more about the financial advisor role, my mind was made. I knew this was the career for me. I knew by getting into this industry, not only would I be able to apply all of the concepts I learned in school, but more importantly, I would be able to help others at the same time.

With little financial discussions as a child, I knew my family had the best intentions, but I quickly realized I would need to turn to other avenues to learn about finance. Yet, I had a hard time finding an information source that wasn't suggesting get rich quick schemes.

This guide aims to be that source for folks from all different backgrounds and education levels. We will be covering some basics that will get everyone on the same page and build on the basics to quite complex strategies for those who have accumulated significant assets.

As I got more involved in the financial services business, I soon realized I had a lot to learn. Luckily, I found some great mentors as I was getting started that sped up the learning curve. Between all the great learning experiences I had, plus a dedicated work ethic, I could see and learn much more than my peers might have in the same time frame.

Here I am in 2020, about ten years into this journey, and I have been waiting for the right time to share my experience, thoughts, trials, and tribulations with you so you can take charge and make a difference in your planning right away. What I have found is that the traditional rules to financial planning have become lazy with the same advice that has been professed since the great depression. We now have more options and nuances to consider than ever before.

It's time to take a more modern, thoughtful approach to financial planning. One that both accounts for your lifestyle goals as well as covers any massive life changes. Through my financial planning career, I wanted to be sure to help families with the discussions to which I was never exposed. This is my best effort to challenge the status quo and provide guidance to develop a retirement by design for anyone and everyone looking to take control.

I am an avid golfer and have been for most of my adult life – although my scores may not show it. I think golf has so many lessons within the game itself that translate so well to life, and in this case, even finances. In golf, it is all about creating a plan and staying within your game, not trying to hit shots or be a hero when you run into situations where you know you may not have the shot needed to execute. Instead, you should focus on a shot you feel comfortable with rather than trying to hit as close to the hole as possible. In finance, creating a game plan is also critical.

When developing a plan, I have seen people time and time again get themselves into trouble by overreaching in their finances and taking on something they may not fully understand at the time. The good news, just like in golf, you can hire your own "financial caddy" in the form of a financial planner to help you navigate the course of personal finance as effectively as possible. In lieu of a direct relationship, it's important to understand every aspect you will run into in developing a thoughtful plan and develop the knowledge in each area, to ensure avoiding overlooked mistakes and taking unnecessary risks.

I promise not to overcomplicate things. I have worked hard to take complex subjects and reduce them into digestible chunks that are immediately actionable. Through my years in working with clients, I have seen how vital simplicity can be as well as the importance of addressing a plan in a more thoughtful approach.

Creating a plan that addresses all aspects and simplifying it down to key areas of focus is where I find the most value. I have seen those who oversimplify and take the advice stating retirement savings is a no brainer and all you have to do is save 10% a year, with no thought to the savings vehicle, fail miserably.

Those following this advice have a hard time finding the "peace of mind" they are looking for because they have no clarity on the future impact of these strategies. Usually, this approach falls short as it lacks structure on how these savings strategies improve that person's life or goals. On the flip side, I have seen clients who have gone to the other end of the spectrum, completely overcomplicating their plan, which led to inaction because things became so overwhelming.

The key theme you will catch throughout this book is creating a plan that includes *purpose*. Most of the advice out there is blanket advice for everyone and does not underscore the value of purpose. I will also give you some specific strategies to act on right away, but the key is to find out the reason for what you are doing and why. If you want to make the most of every strategy or action you take you must understand why you are doing it and understand what that action does to get you even further ahead.

This is not a simple how-to stating that there is some secret sauce or a simple change that will suddenly make all of your dreams come true. I know this type of simple fix advice can seem attractive, and I realize our tendency as humans is to gravitate towards these types of low effort solutions.

But, I want to tell the truth behind what is required. I want to share the strategies I actually use with my clients directly and share how you can use the same strategies to make a significant difference for your future, setting up your ideal life by design in the financial world we live in today.

I. Intro: What is needed in a thoughtful approach to finances?

Everywhere you turn, there is noise around investment and financial planning advice. The good news... the most critical aspect of your retirement planning success is 100% in your control. Through this crash course, my goal is to break apart the old, oversimplified financial advice and share the strategies needed to help you retire successfully and take control in today's world.

The traditional approach:

- Pay off your debt
- Save 10% of your income
- Save all of your assets to your pre-tax 401(k)
- Start with aggressive investments and become more conservative as you are older
- Take Social Security at Full Retirement Age
- Take 4% from your assets in retirement

This can be a great starting point to retirement planning, but in the coming chapters I will share where each of these rules can fall short and how to put yourself in a better position to make the most of your resources, leave a legacy, and retire by design. Today, in 2020, interest rates are at all-time lows, we have many more investment choices than ever before, we are living longer lives, and the definition of retirement has changed significantly.

Planning is never stagnant and always requires ongoing attention. A plane begins flying with a destination's ending coordinates dialed in, and the plane is set on autopilot. It begins in Seattle and flies clear across the country to Miami. The pilot can set the autopilot because they have the destination clearly defined. However, many don't understand that pilot is taking control throughout the flight, making hundreds to thousands of tiny corrections to stay on course. Just a slight wind or a degree off that flight may put the plane in Canada or somewhere in the Caribbean.

The plan is critical, but without the slight manual adjustments over the course of your journey you will never make it to your destination. So, remember to keep referring back to this guide and making corrections as needed. Remember your destination, and remember the plan you established to get you there, then re-evaluate your plan and make those slight adjustments as needed to stay on target. Following a completely rigid financial plan doesn't always work. A meaningful retirement will take some adjustments along the way in order to maximize the resources you have worked so hard for.

Whether you are 30 years old and just getting started towards your retirement, are making final preparations for the next chapter, or already in retirement, planning is vital. Retirement no longer means what it used to. Not too long ago, the average American worked for a company for 30 years until retirement; the company provided a gold watch and a pension and wished you good luck.

Fast forward to 2020, and retirement means many different things to many different folks. Some of us are looking for the old model, hoping to relax in retirement and hang up the coat. Others are working to build a retirement that allows them to work because they want to, not because they have to. They might still plan to work or donate their time to a charity as long as they are physically able to.

There is no right answer. Wherever you find yourself on this spectrum is fine, and the key is to create the plan that gets you where you would like to be. Retirement has changed for the better. We are all living longer and can expect a longer and healthier retirement. But this doesn't come without challenges.

These days, we face a problem that was not around for those before us. While we are in retirement longer, we will also need to provide resources for a longer period of time. For many of us, we may spend more time in "retirement" than we spent working. So, the challenge becomes to make sure we have plans to handle a longer retirement and allow us to create a lifestyle we would like during those years! The strategies we will discuss will share what is needed to prepare for retirement today and make the most of all your resources.

Regardless of what retirement means to you, we must start with the end in mind. The adage stating that by failing to plan, you are planning to fail is 100% true. An engineer always starts a project with the end in mind. They know exactly what they are working to create and back-step from there to determine where to start and the steps need to develop this project.

In planning, if you have a sense of what you are aiming for, you can reverse engineer your ideal life back to what you need to do today. Now, if you are one year from retirement, it may be a bit easier to define than when you are 30 years old and just getting started. However, just like the engineer with a much larger project, even the 30-year-old needs to have an end in mind to allow for easier course-correction along the way.

It is no secret that some of the most successful people in the world work with a plan. They understand the value of tax planning, legacy, and risk management in their lives. They avoid distractions and "quick returns" by staying disciplined and sticking to the plan to achieve their goals.

The key to thoughtful retirement planning comes in four simple steps:

First is to outline your plan: What are you aiming for? All planning starts with clearly defining your goals and priorities. Depending on what you may be willing to give up, you can accomplish all of your dreams or may need to make sacrifices and set priorities to realize the most important goals. Once you have your vision in place, the very first suggestion I have when outlining your plan, DO THE MATH! With anything important you want to achieve in life, don't leave it up to happenstance. Do the math to accomplish your goals, and be sure you can support a life you would like to live in retirement. Don't use others' assumptions; don't simply put together a plan for what your retirement is "supposed" to look like.

Instead, make sure the retirement you are planning is the retirement you have always wanted! Define your ideal retirement. Envision what that would look like, where you would live, what you would do, and what charities you would support. Take the time to find out what these expenses would be and do the math to determine how much you need to save to create this ideal life. This rule applies to all areas in your financial plan and I will be sharing the math needed in each category through the chapters to come. You will thank yourself, and it will be easier to stick to your plan when you can get excited about the future you're building. From there, do the math to determine what is needed to create your actual dream retirement and what you need to do today to get there.

The best place to start, and a rule I am sure we have all heard is to pay yourself first. Now, I believe that if you are younger or in a place where your income is not where you would like it to be, you may consider "paying yourself first" as investing in yourself. Grow your skillset and your ability to bring in more income so you can save even more. Invest in yourself before you invest in anything else. From there, make sure you set aside money as the very first dollars that come from your paycheck to invest for your future.

The good news, if you have a 401(k), the ability to easily pay yourself is already done for you. You just have to take advantage. Once you determine the amount you need to save, this strategy will help you make it there. Those who fail or set up life without choice make decisions based on how they feel.

On the other hand, the most successful and those living a life by design make decisions based on a plan and their future goals. Most of the success in your retirement planning stems from your savings abilities. The investment returns are important, but the most significant impact on your retirement success is your ability to save and invest.

When creating your plan, there are a few key, often-skipped components to consider. A crucial variable involves looking inward. Clearly define what makes you happy and consider money as a vehicle to help you live a fulfilling and happy life. There is so much value in a conversation and proper reflection to consider what components would help make your life better (not things). Create a plan to hit these targets and provide yourself the freedom and ability to accomplish your goals.

Second, you should consider taxation: This will be a huge theme throughout the coming chapters. We will talk about this in length as we dig in, but you need to understand tax trends and the future impacts of tax traps. Determine how taxes fit into the plans you created and find opportunities to minimize your taxes over your entire life. Most of the old approach to tax planning only addresses how to manage taxes once a year, but in today's world, we will be sharing ways to manage your taxation throughout your life to allow yourself more freedom.

Third, take out emotions: This is where most people get in trouble. Do most people stick to their plan, executing on what they need to do to get to retirement? Not exactly. We get nervous in the markets, or worse yet, we find a "can't pass opportunity" claiming ridiculous returns and no risk. Investing is a game of risk and reward. It is easy to get excited about any shiny object that pops up, but we can't let this make us lose track of our plan. We create a plan for a reason. Yet, most people get in trouble trying to chase returns to tell their neighbor or friend at the club how much money they made. Who cares? Predictability and consistency are essential when it comes to a financial plan. You must have the discipline to stay focused. Either the risk is significant for a potential return, or you are paying for it somehow that you may not see.

Sometimes, when doing our financial planning, we may be too close to the subject, and our assumptions may be biased or based on emotion. We often find folks who have taken on planning entirely on their own have strategies around returns, taxes, expenses and more that force them down one path.

Make sure your plan has flexibility mixed into it (more to come later), and I would suggest you use a third party – which could even be a friend – to be sure the assumptions you are using make sense. Use that person to help you develop a plan free of emotions, and more importantly, as an accountability partner to stay on track towards your goals.

Last, you must review and adjust as needed: No plan is ever complete, and you must understand a retirement with purpose is an ongoing endeavor. Once you have outlined your plan, addressed taxation, and put aside emotions, you have created a great foundation to build off. From here, we make adjustments as the winds of life shift.

I am a huge golf fan and play as much as possible, or at least during the three months of sun we get here in the Pacific Northwest. In golf, the best players start with the end in mind, getting the ball in the hole and work backward to develop a strategy for each shot with the understanding that golf is a game of misses and corrections. When a lousy shot happens, the great golfers in the world are able to move forward, put that shot behind them, and reassess what is in front of them now. Things don't always go according to plan, and they understand the importance of flexibility. After a bad shot, they assess the lie and make the best shot they can from their new position, focusing on avoiding compounding mistake after mistake.

Just like golf, in our finances, we must create flexibility and be prepared for adjustments! Create a plan based on our goals, and from there, we can back up to create the most effective plan to get you there. Just as sure as a terrible lie or weather conditions changing your plan in golf, life and your financial goals will change over time. Your personal priorities will change, family dynamics change, markets change, and tax laws change. Some of these you may have control over, while others are entirely out of your hands. Just like the small adjustments made on a golf course to get the best score, your financial planning may need some slight tweaks over time to make sure you are still heading in the right direction.

In finance, we are continually facing unknowns, and a successful financial plan should address these uncertainties allowing you to adjust as needed. When you are forced to make corrections, you must analyze the impact, develop the best strategy possible to weather the storm, and visualize the best shot you can to get back on track.

Once you have your plan in place, remind yourself constantly where you are headed and eliminate the distractions! This doesn't mean you shouldn't change your plan or address changes as needed. Being in this industry long enough, I have seen it all, and time and time again. I have seen even the most thoughtful investors become distracted. I have seen brilliant individuals get off track after hearing about a great new "tip" from their neighbor, completely throwing away all of the hard work they had put in place. There is always a shiny new widget that is the "next big thing" and proposed as a solution to fix all problems. Don't get distracted and buy into these widgets as a solution to all your issues. There is no universal tool in the world of finance.

Advice is everywhere, and there are plenty of rules of thumb out there. The typical, oversimplified approach, in addition to all the distractions we face daily can cause us to lose sight of our target. The norm is to save based on targets for the "Average American" instead of developing your plan for you and creating the life you've always wanted. Let's dig in and start exploring each area you can take a bit more control of today to set yourself up for years of success and a meaningful financial life.

II.   The Basics

The many rules of finance have great intentions, but they often fall short of expectations or leave us with huge blind spots that derail our retirement. While these assumptions can be a helpful start, proper planning in today's world helps you get ahead and make the most of your resources to live a life you have dreamed of as opposed to a life that happens to you.

A very close client experienced the negative impacts of standard retirement rhetoric firsthand. He was a great saver, and a lot of his habits came from his family. His parents were great savers throughout their entire life as well. They did a great job of saving, but they followed the standard advice we all hear, centered upon a low-effort strategy to retire. They saved an emergency fund, put away 10% of their income their whole lives, and had been living under the assumption of a 4% distribution from their assets in retirement. Things were going well until his father was diagnosed with dementia. His father was forced into an assisted living facility while his mother was still at home with the same expenses they had been planning for their whole lives. However, the facility expenses tacked on another $9,000/month to their existing lifestyle expenses to make sure his mom could survive. After only three years in this scenario, and a down market, they found themselves in huge trouble. Not only were they losing a lot of their assets to higher taxes now, but their emergency fund was gone, their savings nearly depleted, and they even found themselves in debt. I know this is scary, but to help avoid this, all you have to do is to follow the strategies we will share and take control of your finances, developing a plan based on you, not the "average American."

Do you want to set up a retirement plan based on what the average saver is doing? A considerable majority of Americans have little to no retirement savings, so you may want to create your own rules around planning instead of following the norm.

To help you design your ideal retirement, I want to spend some time defining some basics. Like any effective financial plan, you must start with a strong foundation to build on. There are some basic terms and strategies that come up every day in finance that we will define as a foundation for the concepts to build off. You may know some of them like the back of your hand while others you laugh off and hope the topic is changed. Here is your chance to brush up on these baseline items and set a strong financial foundation for yourself. We will be touching on many of these terms throughout this chapter and will highlight any new terms as they come up throughout the book.

Have you thought about how you might define the difference between saving and investing? This slight discrepancy can mean a world of difference in your planning. When I start my week with some healthy meal prepping, I create a few meals and put them in the fridge. I am *saving* these meals for a future date. I do not expect to see more food or experience any growth in these meals unless I leave them in there too long! This is savings. When we put money in the bank or hold cash, we are saving it for the future without expecting the asset to grow. The idea is to know the funds will be available if we need them.

The challenge? With the world we live in, we are going backward year-to-year as inflation erodes the value of those hard-earned dollars. Think of it this way, with modern inflation, the meals I prepare and put in my fridge have less food in them by the time I'm ready to eat. It is essential to have some level of savings, but savings alone will not get you any further ahead in your finances and has no chance of creating freedom for your future. This is why we invest. When *investing*, we are putting money into an asset with the goal of growth in the future. The goal here is to create more money out of existing capital. Now when we add in opportunity for growth, we are also introducing the idea of *risk*. There are all levels of risk, you must understand and find your comfort zone, but everyone must be willing to take on some level of risk in investing, or they may find they can never get ahead due to inflation.

Inflation is something that I find significantly underestimated. When evaluating investment choices, the impact of inflation should be a big factor in determining how to invest and what those returns may mean. If anybody is lucky enough to remember when movie tickets only cost $5 for the matinee show, you know what I am talking about. Now those same movie tickets can be near $20. THIS IS INFLATION.

Now you may hear a lot about inflation running around 2% per year which is something they call the consumer price index, or CPI.

The challenge with the CPI measure of inflation is that it includes a basket of goods that may not be all so timely in what we are buying today – and doesn't include things like healthcare costs. So, for inflation assumptions, it may be wise to consider a bit higher figure to help provide a bit more slush in case you find your expenses running at a higher inflation rate.

Investments

Now that we have introduced the concept of inflation and savings vs. investing, it is critical to understand some of the broad categories of assets we can invest in. The first is *cash*. Cash assets would fall under the savings category mentioned above. The benefit of keeping cash is we know it will be there and cash does not have the typical risk we associate with investments. We can rely on that dollar we put under the mattress being there when we need it – unless the kids find your rainy-day funds!

The risk of having too much in savings is exactly what we had discussed with inflation. Although we can rely on that dollar being there for us, we are going backward as inflation slowly makes that dollar worth less and less over time.

So, when we start investing, we explore asset classes that introduce other types of risk. If we are looking for a bit more return with some stability, we may look to bond investments. A **bond** is simply an instrument of debt. When you buy a bond, you are essentially loaning money to some government, state, municipality, or company. You may loan these organizations money under the assumption that they pay you a certain amount of interest each year for borrowing your assets.

The bond market is vast and much larger than the stock market. But for simplicity's sake, as you might imagine, there may be less risk in loaning money to the U.S. government (that might get some chuckles) as opposed to John's lawnmower shack next door. The benefit of bonds is we start to introduce a bit of return into the picture while still maintaining some stability. The challenge is those interest payments are only as strong as the issuer of the debt. With bonds, we have a risk that the person we are loaning money to may not be able to pay us back.

When we want to explore growth options, one of the most common areas we look at is **stocks** or equities. When we purchase a share in a company's stock, we are essentially buying ownership of that particular company. That means, for better or worse, we will participate and are invested in that company's future. If the company does well, we may realize great returns for our investment. If that company does poorly, we may recognize losses in our assets due to their share price. Stocks are an excellent opportunity to experience growth and outpace inflation for long term goals. Still, we need to understand the risks involved

Correlation describes the relationship between two investments. If two assets are heavily correlated, they move in lockstep with one another. For assets that are negatively correlated, they move in opposition.

with the companies we invest in as now we introduce market and volatility risk leading to up and down movement in your investment over time.

When exploring diversification (more to come soon) opportunities in the new world, we may introduce *alternative assets*. When we say alternatives, think real estate, art, etc. These particular assets are not tied directly to stock market volatility and generally are not correlated to market returns directly.

However, alternatives typically are not very liquid. If you own real estate, you may not be able to pull off some of the siding and sell it if an emergency were to come up. A great way to think of alternatives is similar to running a retail business. If you opened a storefront selling winter coats, the busy season would likely be the fall and winter months.

Now, if you start selling swimsuits, your busy season for these goods will fall in spring and summer. Being the smart business owner you are, you think, well what if I also decide to sell toothbrushes? For these goods, the season most likely won't have a direct impact on your sales. If you think of stocks and bonds as coats and swimsuits, you can see that typically these goods sell at different times. When sales of one good are up, the other is down.

This actually means they have a negative correlation to one another – they move in opposition. Alternatives can act as the toothbrush in your investment portfolio. This doesn't mean these assets are always up, but the toothbrush sales are not directly impacted by coats or swimsuit sales – meaning they do not correlate. This illustrates how alternatives can act as an asset that may not correlate to the performance in your stock and bond holdings, allowing for more diversification.

Diversification and Asset Allocation

As we discuss different asset classes, it's essential to understand a few principles when building your portfolio. Two very key fundamentals are diversification and asset allocation. Both refer to the mix of assets in your portfolio, but many times these are seen as one in the same. So how do we define these two terms? I might suggest some simple definitions to explain the difference between the two. Ideally, your investment portfolio may have money in all types of different asset classes. Let's say you have Investor A and Investor B, who both have a portfolio of five different funds.

Investor A	Investor B
XYZ Large Cap Fund	XYZ Large Cap Fund
ABC US Growth Fund	ABC Mid Cap Growth fund
Alphabets US Large Companies	Small Companies Fund of America
US Growth Fund of America	Europacific Growth fund
S&P 500 Index Fund	Bond Index Fund

This and the following chart are hypothetical examples and for illustrative purposes only. No specific investments or funds were used in this example.

Who would you consider is diversified? On the surface, you may say both are diversified. The challenge is that although Investor A has different funds, all of this investor's funds are the same and they probably own the same assets. I would suggest Investor B is certainly more diversified, as this investor has different asset classes that may not move all in lockstep at the same time (non-correlated assets).

Under the old definitions, many folks felt they needed to invest with different advisors or different custodians to be diversified. With some thought, it's clear this is not the meaning of diversification. In fact, you may find both advisors hold the same things and aren't any better off, not to mention the advisors have a hard time not knowing the other side of the picture.

Simply put, **diversification** refers to the spreading of assets across different types of assets. Now, do either of these investors have proper asset allocation? We have no idea because we don't have percentages showing how much is in each asset.

Investor A		Investor B	
XYZ Large Cap Fund	5%	XYZ Large Cap Fund	40%
ABC Mid Cap Growth fund	5%	ABC Mid Cap Growth fund	10%
Small Companies Fund of America	80%	Small Companies Fund of America	10%
Europacific Growth fund	5%	Europacific Growth fund	10%
Bond Index Fund	5%	Bond Index Fund	30%

Here we bring back two investors, both with diversified portfolios, but who is appropriately allocated? The answer is a bit less clear as the proper allocation should change over time, given risks and valuations as the economy shifts. That said, in this extreme example, it is probably safe to say Investor B has a more effective asset allocation. **Asset allocation** defines the amount we put into each of our diversified asset classes. Keep in mind that this is not a recommendation for an allocation but rather an illustration to share the difference. Your allocation really should change over time, and we will touch on this more as we get into more advanced concepts.

There are two themes around investment strategies. Tactical allocation refers to the timely changes you may make based on market fluctuations whereas strategic allocation refers to the long-term static allocation.

It's funny that when I first began my career, I believed in day trading. I thought I was going to make people rich overnight with trading –

it's so simple, right? It doesn't take long from personal experiences and watching colleagues to realize what works and what doesn't. A thoughtful portfolio with proper diversification and slight **tactical** tweaks in asset allocation over time is what drives dependable, long term success.

Taxation

Let's switch gears and take a minute to discuss the various ways accounts are taxed. Not too long ago, we didn't have much choice in our retirement savings vehicles. Today, we have many options and different tax implications to these choices as well.

The first question to explore is not what to invest in, but what type of account to invest in. Any investment has three layers; you have the outermost layer which we will be talking about here – the "tax wrapper" that dictates how your account will be taxed. Then you have the hard candy shell. This covers the platform you are choosing to invest in (401(k), brokerage accounts, annuities, etc.). Lastly, you would have the soft chewy center, this is the actual investments themselves (the stocks, bonds, etc. we discussed above). For now, let's focus on the tax wrapper. This will be extremely important and something we will build on repeatedly in the chapters to come, so be sure you understand this well.

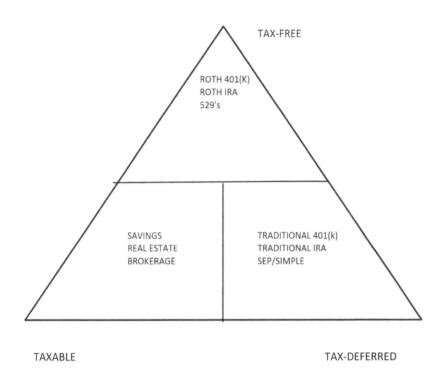

TAX-FREE

ROTH 401(K)
ROTH IRA
529's

SAVINGS   TRADITIONAL 401(k)
REAL ESTATE   TRADITIONAL IRA
BROKERAGE   SEP/SIMPLE

TAXABLE   TAX-DEFERRED

What you see in the chart outlines the three different ways any investment is taxed. In the bottom left section, you will see taxable accounts. Think about these accounts as vehicles that you are investing dollars in that have already been taxed. The contributions may be coming from income after taxes or from your savings or checking account. These vehicles are "taxed as you go," meaning you may pay taxes annually based on any account activity. If you receive interest or dividends, you may pay taxes on that amount for the year. If you bought a stock at $20 and sold it later at $30, you may pay taxes the year of sale as capital gains. We will come back to capital gains in detail when we dig into the tax planning chapter.

For now, it's essential to understand that capital gains rates are usually a lower, flat tax rate for any profits you recognize on an investment. The challenge with taxable accounts is that we do not get any direct tax benefits. Because we do not recognize these direct tax benefits, there are no limitations in your ability to use this type of account; income does not affect your ability to invest, and there are no limits to how much can be invested, how long the money must be invested, or when you have to take money out.

Next, you will notice the tax-deferred bucket. For example, think of your traditional 401(k)s, IRAs etc. Generally, we may get a deduction for the dollars invested today, and this money goes in pre-tax. Now, as the account grows, rather than paying taxes year to year, all the dividends, earnings, and growth are deferred no matter how much you buy or sell.

The trade-off is that when we take money out in retirement, every single dollar we pull out is fully taxable as ordinary income. As you might imagine, this is typically where we find a HUGE majority of people's assets in retirement. The challenge is then that all these assets are taxable. What if an emergency comes up or a major medical bill? A new expense may increase our income for the year and therefore our taxes. Not only will you be taxed on these accounts, but generally, you will be forced to take distributions from this type of account later in life. We will discuss both of these considerations in much more detail in future chapters.

Last, we have "tax-free." Now bear with me a bit; nothing is really tax-free. What this is referring to is the growth in these accounts is tax-free. The contributions into this account are non-deductible, but as it grows and when we get to a point where we take money out of this account, all qualified distributions are 100% tax-free!

So, think about this as the tax-deferred vehicle flipped upside down. Would you rather pay taxes now on your dollars or in the future? We will share more thoughts on this to come but the benefit of this vehicle is we have an entirely tax-free asset when we get to retirement. However, there may be limitations to take advantage of these Roth vehicles based on income, savings rates, etc.

Many employers may offer retirement plans, typically in the form of a 401(k). Generally, these vehicles may allow for tax-deferral and

Roth options, plus will allow you to save a fair amount of your paycheck towards a retirement account. When you leave your employer, or if your income qualifies, you may also establish your own IRA by moving these funds, which is a personal retirement account. Employers in the non-profit space may have different versions of the 401(k) but, generally speaking, the taxation of these accounts is the same.

If you do find yourself with a 401(k) or any of its brothers and sisters in the company retirement plan space, the very first step is to be sure you take advantage of any available match! Most often, a company will match your retirement savings up to a certain dollar amount or percentage. If nothing else, be sure to find this limit and contribute at least enough to take advantage of this free money.

For instance, let's say a company offers a dollar for dollar match up to 5%. If you contribute 5% to your plan, the company will "match" your contribution and contribute the precise amount to your account for your future use. This company match means, for every dollar you put in, you get an instant, 100% guaranteed match on your initial contribution. Of course, the investments you choose may dictate your returns after the initial contribution, but there is nowhere else you will be able to find the type of immediate, initial return an employer match may provide, so please be sure to take advantage.

Pensions

Some of you may even have a portion of your retirement through a pension vehicle. Keep in mind the taxation of this will be the same as your pre-tax 401(k) assets, and you will be taxed as you take your distributions. The taxation is set, but you will find there are many different ways to elect your benefit.

You may find you have a lump sum option, a lifetime income option, and a survivorship option (there are other variations and combinations of distribution options, but for this purpose we will keep it simple). The lump-sum option may allow you to take a one-time, total, distribution benefit that can be rolled out into an IRA. If you feel you don't need the guarantees a pension provides or would like to take control of the asset directly, this may be a good way to take the asset and create your own income stream. However, you will no longer receive any guarantees from the company.

The lifetime income option will allow you to take a monthly benefit for the rest of your life as long as you live. The great thing about a lifetime benefit is you know you will receive an income just from waking up out of bed each month. The challenge is that you have no control over changing the amount or ability to go back to the well to take more in times where you need additional funds. Also, if you are married, this benefit may not continue to your spouse at your passing.

For those concerned about maintaining benefits for their spouses, **ERISA** requires that survivorship options be available. If you choose a survivorship option, you may receive a slightly lower monthly income, but the benefits will be guaranteed to pay out for as long as either you or your spouse live. It will pay a benefit until the last of you pass away.

> Employee Retirement Income Security Act of 1974 (ERISA) is a law that sets minimum standards for most established retirement plans

Sometimes you may see variations with 100% of the benefit continued to your spouse, down to even 50%, but this will impact the benefit amount during your life. The more that continues to your spouse, the less you can expect while you are living. Survivorship options can be great because now we know both ourselves and our spouses will have a monthly income throughout our lives. However, the challenges remain that we may not have much access to the benefit or flexibility when life comes at us.

A pension is essentially a company-sponsored version of an annuity. Some of those without pensions may consider an annuity as a way to create a guaranteed income source. Just be aware of the liquidity issues we shared above and be mindful that annuities often may come with higher costs or limited investment options to provide you the guarantees. The guarantees associated with annuities are only as strong as the company issuing the contract, so you need to consider other risks as a part of these decisions as well. (This level of detail is beyond the context of this text.)

Mutual and Exchange Traded Funds

After understanding the tax implications and platforms available, we can move on to the chewy center (or the actual investments). When investing, one of the first places people turn when looking for diversification is **mutual funds** or **exchange-traded funds** (ETFs). The best way I can explain a mutual fund or ETF is a basket of stocks or bonds. With one fund, you can find instant access to many holdings. Especially for those just starting, this can give a great chance to find diversification where you may not be able to typically based on your account size by purchasing individual stocks, given their share price.

For instance, if you are starting as an investor with $3,000 to invest, you may only be able to invest in one share of Amazon stock.

However, with the same $3,000, you can invest in an **S&P 500** ETF or a mutual fund that instantly gives you exposure to 500 different companies. For those who can use individual stocks, these funds can be great core portfolio positions, allowing you to round out the portfolio with exposure to individual stocks, bonds, or sectors for a bit more spice or to work toward your goals more effectively.

The S&P 500 refers to an index within the stock market. In order to compare, indices were created as benchmarks or measuring sticks to track the movement of different market segments. These days you are able to buy a fund that mirrors an entire index within one fund and own all 500 companies within this particular index.

The Rule of 72

Now that we understand how and where we can invest, I want to share a helpful concept to keep in mind as you read through future chapters.

One constructive theory is something called the **rule of 72**. The rule gives us a great, quick example of how money can work for us. The exercise is far from perfect but can allow you to very quickly determine how long it will take for your money to double. The rule goes as follows; take an expected rate of return (say 6%) and divide this into 72; e.g., 72/6=12.

So, if you were to find an investment that produced a 6% rate of return, your money would double in 12 years. Let's assume a 12% rate of return, well now we can double our money in only six years, we just cut the doubling period in half (although almost certainly took on more risk to get here). Now let's look at current interest rates in the bank and assume a .5% interest rate which is great at this particular time, 72/.5= 144! Yes, it would take 144 years for your money to double in the bank! Now, where would you like your long-term assets to sit? You may already have some thoughts, but we will be sure to get into more detail as we go.

Rate of return	Doubling Period (In Years)
12%	6
10%	7.2
8%	9
6%	12
4%	18
2%	36
And for fun... 0.50%	144

Now that we have some basics, we can start to build on these principles moving forward to break down the traditional advice we've always heard and break through towards building our ideal retirement. If you have areas in this chapter you don't fully understand, go back and re-read to embrace each topic as everything else we discuss will build off of this chapter. Now that you're ready, let's get into the heavy lifting.

III. Identifying and Categorizing Expenses

Don't worry, this is not a how-to on the b-word in finance (budgeting). In fact, I may be one of few planners who will tell you a detailed budget may not be as helpful as common knowledge may lead you to believe. The traditional version of budgeting typically outlines a plan to track your expenses to the penny so you can find ways to cut costs. I feel a new approach to budgeting is important because I feel this outdated approach to a budget is similar to the latest diet fad. When we put ourselves on an overly strict diet, we ALWAYS fall back on our old habits.

The target is far too strict and radical to be able to make a complete 180. Similarly, with a budget, telling you not to spend $5 on a cup of coffee will only lead to falling back on your old habits, and typically that coffee is not the issue. It's the habit of saving first that is more important. That said, I will suggest a budgeting 2.0 that we will outline, providing an idea of what you spend and some of the larger categories you spend on to be sure your money is going where you would like it to.

Budgeting 2.0: A New Approach

The most significant difference in this modern approach to a budget is to break out your expenses in needs and wants. Knowing what you need to survive and having an idea of what you spend for leisure will allow you to create your dream retirement with more thought to the design.

Unfortunately, expense categories are essential when discussing planning, and this chapter will serve as a framework for everything we discuss in the chapters to come. Especially with retirement, you must look before you leap! Trying to develop a financial plan with absolutely zero thought to expenses can be a death sentence. You must know what you are getting yourself into before you make the jump.

Needs

What might be an example of a needed expense? I am sure we can all think of a few right off the bat; housing, food, water, utilities, taxes (unfortunately). There are many more that would all into this category as well but breaking out your needs is critical in creating a thoughtful retirement plan. We will address why this is so important in our distribution planning chapter in detail, but as a hint, this is our guaranteed income target.

For now, the importance of this number is key. Knowing what you need to survive every month is extremely important. Such knowledge can help you determine things like emergency fund levels and other risk management pieces to assess your risks, making sure you can make do if something happened to your income.

Wants

What might be a good example of an expense we would call a want? Wants may include traveling, eating out, and although arguably a need for me, golf would fall into this category. This portion of your expenses is likely to fluctuate and probably change over time based on your lifestyle and hobbies as you grow and try new things.

Wants gives us a sense of the "fun stuff" we are working towards in retirement. We didn't work so hard all our lives just to pay bills; we need to have fun too. Outlining these expenses allows us to develop a plan to create the income to handle these expenses.

Needs	Current		Retirement	
Shelter	$	2,000.00	$	2,000.00
Food	$	600.00	$	600.00
Utilities	$	200.00	$	200.00
Taxes	$	2,500.00	$	2,000.00
Insurances	$	300.00	$	1,000.00
Basic Internet/Cable	$	50.00	$	50.00
Golf?				
Total Needs	$	5,650.00	$	5,850.00
Wants				
Travel	$	500.00	$	1,000.00
Entertainment	$	300.00	$	600.00
Dining Out	$	400.00	$	400.00
Toys	$	250.00	$	250.00
Gifts	$	100.00	$	200.00
Premium Internet/Cable	$	200.00	$	200.00
Golf....	$	400.00	$	800.00
Total Wants	$	2,150.00	$	3,450.00
Total Expenses	$	7,800.00	$	9,300.00

The key when breaking out your expenses is to create your own definitions of needs and wants based on your values. There is no right or wrong answer, the most important factor is that it reflects the life you want to live. Once we can define these categories, it will also allow us to reward ourselves more often and guilt-free! We now can freely spend more in our "wants" categories when we make more money. This ability to spend freely applies to both the accumulation and distribution phases of retirement. Should we receive a major bonus, close a big deal, or receive a pay raise for our production during our working years, we should reward ourselves for these accomplishments.

On the flip side, when in retirement, if any of these apply or the markets simply have a great year for your investments, you can freely spend on that extra trip or some nice meals out with the family. Just don't fall in the rat race trap by making this a reoccurring expense that has now become a part of a more expensive lifestyle and be sure we don't spend more than the bonus noticed that year! We want to do our best to avoid falling into a trap where credit card interest becomes part of our expense breakdown.

Time and time again, I have seen clients gearing up for retirement and compromising their retirement to fit into their savings. Let's reverse this train of thought. Let's make your savings fit to create the retirement you have always dreamed of. We didn't work so hard our whole lives to make compromises. This is not the goal. Don't negotiate your dreams or you may find yourself in trouble a few years into retirement when you realize your expense assumptions were only addressing the needs because you felt you could make it work. Retirement should be enjoyed, so be honest with yourself and be sure to include the wants you are aiming for.

Often, I have seen assumptions where the person based their plan on lower expenses in retirement. Unfortunately, when these folks come to me, it's too late. Many times, they have been forced back out of retirement. We can avoid this, and it starts by honestly outlining your retirement expenses in these two categories.

Earlier I mentioned I am not a huge believer in traditional budgets. While I maintain that position, I believe there is a new and fundamental way to budget. By giving a rough idea of what you spend in these categories on an annual basis, this allows you to plan around some of these factors for savings and future income purposes. Don't feel that you will need to cut out your "wants" when you practice this exercise. The purpose of living is to enjoy life today, and I would not suggest you cut out these expenses. This baseline gives you a better understanding of your risks and opportunities while you are in your savings years and how you may structure your income in your distribution years (more to come on this soon). If you know that your needs are roughly $5k/month, you very quickly can assess what you would need to be able to handle if you were to lose your job or become sick or injured.

With this insight, you can create strategies to be sure you can handle these expenses for a period of time without being kicked out of house and home when you experience life's challenges. During your accumulation years, knowing your expenses can help assess your cash flow and explore more savings opportunities. I don't think anyone should give up paying for a coffee if it makes them happy and is something they enjoy in life. I know this may save you money over time, but maybe the coffee once a week makes you happier than the impact of the extra $20/month savings. What I do believe in, is an objective understanding of what these costs are for you. Then, as you explore your plan and what you want to accomplish, you will have a baseline of a decision to determine if giving up that coffee is really going to get you where you want to be – or if there may be some other way to still accomplish your goals.

During your distribution years, these categories are paramount to a successful income strategy. We will be covering this in detail in the retirement distribution chapter next, but having this outlined will dictate a considerable aspect of your planning strategies in retirement. Now let's tie this all together.

IV.   Retirement Income Planning

If you get anything out of this reading, focus on this chapter and the tax planning chapter. Nearly all the articles, books, tools, calculators only tell you how much to save based on a simple analysis that you can take 4% of your assets, and it should last 30 years. But

> The 4% Rule: This was a rule of thumb created to determine what distribution rate you may be able to take from your assets in retirement.

will this old rule of thumb really solve all your planning considerations?

Of course, this all comes from the biggest question on everyone's mind: *how much money do I need to retire?*

To you, this is probably no surprise, but this is the single biggest question I run into as a financial planner. Simply saving towards a net worth target is one of the most common mistakes I see regarding retirement planning. In the new world, the amount of your nest egg is not the only factor in your retirement success. We have more strategies available to us as investors than ever before.

It's therefore critical to understand the primary factors of retirement success: the income you can generate, your ability to handle surprises, and how your nest egg may be taxed (as you will see in the next figure may have a significant impact on your distribution needs). As a starting point, we will discuss how to create income and considerations for your portfolio as you move into retirement. We will then return to the unexpected and taxation in the chapters to come.

	Investor A (From IRA)	Investor B (From Roth)
Distribution	$ 123,788.00	$ 100,000.00
Taxes	$ 23,788.00	$ -
Net Dist.	$ 100,000.00	$ 100,000.00

I promise I am not trying to deflect, but the amount of money in our nest egg is not the only factor in a successful retirement. Just as substantial is what you do when you actually get to retirement. The common belief is that retirement is all about getting to the peak. This idea suggests that the hard work and focus are behind us once we reach retirement and all media and investment firms seem to solely focus on the first half of this equation.

Generally, 60% of a retiree's income comes from portfolio gains while IN retirement, only 30% comes from gains while the person was working, and only 10% from contributions. So, why would we stop focusing on our retirement planning when we get to retirement?

In fact, these figures really show that the strategies you incorporate become even more valuable while in your retirement years. Anybody who knows mountain climbing, or even those who don't, know that it isn't climbing the mountain that presents the challenge, it's coming down. Coming down the mountain, a climber becomes tired and can let up on their focus, becoming lazy. The same applies to retirement.

Saving and accumulating is not easy, but it can be the more straightforward half of the equation, yet many folks think that there is no more planning to be done once they make it to retirement. As a retiree, it can be easy to lose sight of your plan and feel you've made it. Such distraction will lead to disaster; as we become complacent with our planning, we lose focus and look up one day, realizing that we need to go back to work. This focus solely on the accumulation phase isn't your fault; it is what the media and financial institutions have led you to believe. So, perhaps the better question to ask is,

"How do I create the most effective income stream to make the most of my resources?"

Wherever you are in your savings journey, when it comes to retirement planning, the very first step is to take inventory of all your accounts and assets.

> *I was working with a client recently, and the first step in our planning process was precisely this: taking the inventory. The client was looking solid in retirement but needed more savings to allow for flexibility. They were able to handle their lifestyle expenses, but if there was an unexpected expense or tax rates were changed, they may have found themselves in a difficult position. Through this inventory process, we were able to identify a document that, previously, the client hadn't paid much attention to. The document was from an investment company, but this client, let's call her Mrs. Jackson, didn't think anything of it. Luckily, we caught this and thought it would be worth looking into further as it was very possible this was an abandoned account. After some digging, we found out not only did Mrs. Jackson have an account out in the abyss, but this account was worth nearly $200,000.00. By taking the time to dig in and explore every angle, we could find these extra funds. This made a difference for this particular client, allowing them the additional flexibility to retire immediately if they wanted.*

Income

After taking inventory, the key to successful retirement planning today is developing an income strategy out of your assets. The distribution phase can be so challenging because the focus completely shifts from accumulation to distribution. Yet most of our portfolios remain similar or may become slightly less "risky." But what does that mean, and why do we do this? Your portfolio's primary purpose in retirement is to create income!

There are many ways to address this, but I would encourage you to develop an income strategy within your portfolio to help accomplish the goal rather than simply selling out of your positions to create the cash when you need it. The old approach may have been to simply sell assets as needed to provide for your expenses. Instead, in today's world, you can give yourself a huge leg up by starting to explore how much income your portfolio can create through fixed income and/or stock dividends to line up with those expenses.

Now, you should not entirely shift to an income ONLY strategy either, it is still imperative to have the right balance in assets between the different asset classes to allow for growth, keep up with inflation, and minimize the impact of volatility. For those further out, we may be able to handle market swings better, and our portfolio may be more growth-oriented because of this, but as we get closer and closer, we may need to shift our stance with the end game in mind.

Investments in Retirement

When we move into retirement, we no longer have an employer providing a paycheck for us. It is critical to adjust our mindset to developing this income stream for ourselves. I have seen so many people get to retirement and decide to put all of their assets in cash, hoping this will solve these income problems. However, what is the challenge with this? If you remember the first chapter, one of the "risks" with cash is inflation. Simply based on the government measure of inflation (not including health care, etc.), your dollar in the bank may be worth at least 2% less every single year as the costs of living increases.

The structure of your portfolio needs to take a shift as you gear up and move into retirement. It is still critical to own some stock positions in your portfolio to keep up with future inflation and offset the challenges of a cash and bond-only portfolio.

If you still own stocks (which I suggest you do), those stocks may shift from growth companies to value companies that pay dividends (helping to create income). You may move some of your stock or equity exposure to other assets that may still be "risky" but allow you to drive income. You may even consider new asset classes, such as real estate, to enable you to drive more income. I am sure it is clear now, but the game quickly becomes income, income, income, but we still need to be sure we have a well-diversified portfolio. If you are further out from retirement, understanding the target by focusing on your specific income goal will help you develop your retirement savings strategies and understand how things may translate into income in retirement.

How To Handle Market Swings

When you transition into retirement, be prepared. We have touched on the importance of keeping stock positions in today's world, but this doesn't come without the markets' ups and downs. Suddenly, you will notice market swings hurt much more. During the distribution phase, not only do we feel a more considerable concern for market swings and develop more angst, but the truth is, it's justified. These market swings do have a much larger impact leading up to, and in retirement. Imagine yourself recently retired, you have worked for 30 years to save up this nest egg that will allow you to move forward, but it MUST last your entire life.

As you are taking distributions, the markets run into a tough cycle for a few months and you notice the value of your portfolio drops. Because you are taking money out while the market is also dropping quickly, you can probably already feel the angst this may cause and might even imagine how this impacts you financially. As the next diagram shows, if the markets drop by 25%, it will take a 50% return to get back to where you started and taking money out of your accounts makes these downturns even larger (more cash is coming out and assets sold at a discount).

When you are in the accumulation phase, and the market drops, you are at least buying low with the contributions you are regularly making. However, closer to our retirement date and when taking distributions, when the market drops, most find themselves selling low to create the income they need. This is not what we want to do. We want to buy low and sell high! Taking the time to determine your allocation, addressing risk, and creating a thoughtful/flexible plan in creating income from your portfolio is critical to help you prepare for this change in mindset AND the change in strategy associated with taking money out. When in retirement, risk management becomes much more important. Remember when we were kids and we would have the bowling alley put up the bumpers to help us hit the target easier? Adding some risk management "bumpers" to your retirement portfolio can have huge impacts to your sanity and your income.

Returns	Investor A	Returns	Investor B
	$100,000		$100,000
-50%	$50,000	-25%	$75,000
50%	$75,000	50%	$112,500

The Bucket Approach

To add bumpers to your retirement portfolio, it helps to have a diversified portfolio. The nuts and bolts may remain the same but may require an update from steel materials to titanium to provide the most sturdy version based on the times. One of the best ways to address your portfolio as a whole is to think in terms of buckets.

When you make a giant stew in a crockpot, you put some in a bowl to eat right now, some into containers to save for tomorrow, and some may go in the freezer to keep for a rainy day. You can create a three-bucket system within your one portfolio (or being creative, based on each account's tax nuances). The idea is to create bucket one for your expenses today, which would consist of cash and cash-like alternatives. The idea here is extremely low risk and maximum liquidity.

Bucket two can be to drive the income to fill up bucket one. Here is where you find your traditional bond asset classes. If you are less risk-averse, maybe stocks that pay dividends fall in here too. Many of the positions you hold in retirement may pay out capital gains when a fund has a good year, you may own mutual funds which own stocks that pay dividends, and your bond positions most likely pay interest to you. Most investors have dividends and income from their portfolio holdings reinvested in the assets automatically. Gearing up and into retirement, you should change this so each of these respective categories will pay to cash, helping to create and refill our first bucket of cash and short-term reserves.

Lastly, the third bucket is for growth to help handle inflation concerns. If you are 65 when you retire, you may have 30 years or more to make your money last. If all we are doing is creating income and keeping cash, you will have a hard time dealing with inflation. So, bucket three is designed to be the stock or equity portion of your portfolio, allowing you to have a piece growing to not only keep up with inflation but grow for future use or potential inheritance.

As you might imagine, depending on your level of assets and expenses, one may be able to afford – or need to be – riskier than others, either to grow their assets to "catch up" or to leave more for the next generation or charity of their choosing. For those early in the accumulation phase, you may be able to stomach more risk than those who are ten years or less away from retirement.

Needs and Wants

In the last chapter, we broke out expenses into needs and wants. This next step in retirement planning will help your distribution strategies and determine how much may need to go into your different buckets. I grew up playing hockey, but a quote we all know very well from The Great One, Wayne Gretzky, once said, "I skate to where the puck is going to be." Use this mindset to address planning.

Develop strategies based on where you would like to be, not where you are today. Separating your expenses is so important to help you create an income plan when you no longer have a paycheck coming in each month. Once you have the expenses broken out into needs and wants, you want to match these expenses with the appropriate income sources. Whether 20 years from retirement or two years into your retirement phase, I guarantee these expenses will change, but having a clear strategy today makes these changes so much easier to adjust to with a strong baseline in place.

Match up your "needs" with "guaranteed" income sources. A guaranteed income source may be Social Security (don't laugh!), pensions, annuities, real estate income, or a fixed income strategy from bonds. The source details aren't as crucial as matching up so that you can cover your needs out of "guaranteed" sources. We will discuss Social Security and other guaranteed sources in much more detail later. Still, the whole idea here is to ensure that no matter what happens in the market you know your living expenses are taken care of, creating the freedom to keep you fed and in house and home.

Once we have matched our needs with guaranteed sources, we can bring in and match our wants (the fun stuff) with the more flexible investments, such as our traditional investment portfolios, cash, stocks, etc. We didn't work for 30 years busting our butts to save just to survive. Now that we know our needs are taken care of, you can feel much better knowing a shift in the market won't kick you out of house and home. These asset classes are subject to volatility and market risk, but when these assets are funding our wants, a bad year in the market may simply mean one less trip or that you cannot get those brand-new golf clubs! 😊 On the flip side, when the markets are up, you can plan to spend a bit more on the wants, the areas you enjoy and worked so hard to save towards.

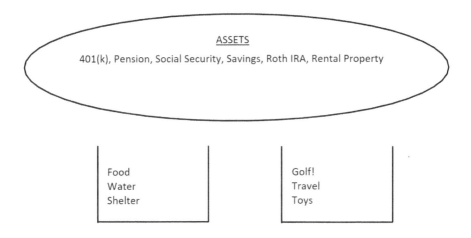

As we discussed, the biggest mistake we see in retirement planning comes from the media's primary focus on accumulation. To create a life by design, the distribution phase needs some attention. Given that 60% of retirees' measurable income returns come from the period in retirement these days, it is critical to spend time focusing on these distribution strategies and to avoid mistakes.

By breaking out your expenses into categories, matching up your needs and wants with proper income streams, and shifting from a growth strategy to one that accomplishes your income and growth needs, you will have a solid framework for your distribution plan! Continue to review your strategies year after year to adjust as life, goals, economies, or tax laws shift. Now that we have developed a strategy to handle our expenses, we also need to prepare for the unexpected.

V.   Unexpected Expenses

Now that we have covered our known expenses, it's critical to take the unexpected into account. And in a time where many of us may be in retirement longer than we were working, you can certainly expect some curveballs along the way.

The one guarantee in planning is that nothing will go according to your plan. While we use our goals as a baseline for the planning assumptions, it can be easy to assume all is covered. Be careful falling into this trap as a massive part of what we do as financial planners is to create as many different paths as possible – allowing you the flexibility to handle any changes in your plan and still come out strong. A part of any thoughtful plan is to account for unexpected expenses, a part is tax planning, and a part is addressing risks nobody may be able to foresee.

Much of the traditional advice you hear helps you save towards a target, assuming everything goes exactly according to plan. This is critical as a starting point, but if you don't have some wiggle room in your planning, one unexpected expense can derail everything you have worked so hard for.

Many times, the unexpected can be the biggest curveball in retirement. Although we categorize them as "unexpected," we can all plan with relative certainty that we will run into these speed bumps at some point in our retirement lifespan. Unexpected expenses can hit us in many different forms.

From healthcare expenses to long-term care costs, a new roof, to kids knocking on the front door needing help. Without any clarity on exactly when and what these costs may be, it is critical to have a plan and some slush in our strategies to accommodate, allowing us the ability to bob and weave to avoid the punches.

Medical Costs

The most common unexpected expenses we see include medical costs, housing costs, tax law changes, and of course, long-term care expenses. One of these expenses that becomes a large portion of a retiree's outflows are healthcare costs. The average retiree spends nearly $300k in healthcare costs throughout their retirement. To help with these expenses, we are eligible for a government program around health care called Medicare.

> Long Term Care expenses refer to costs associated with the need of assistance in daily living and oftentimes are not covered by standard medical insurance.

Medicare

At age 65, we become eligible for **Medicare**, which allows us to enroll in an insurance program when most of us may not have as many options after leaving our employer. We will not be digging into every detail around Medicare, but there are some key pieces to understand. There are four parts to Medicare.

The first is Part A which is the free form of Medicare. If you are already receiving social security benefits, you will be automatically enrolled in Medicare Part A, otherwise you need to be sure to enroll at 65. The Part A portion provides a baseline coverage which really doesn't cover a whole lot except a bed for a short period of time if you are very sick.

Part B is where you begin to round out your plan and get a bit more coverage. This portion's cost is relatively inexpensive but still doesn't cover everything you may be used to, and premiums may vary based on your income.

Then we have Part C, or Medicare Advantage plans, which feel more like the medical insurance you are used to. Part C can be the most expensive portion of your Medicare costs because it includes the most coverage. There are plans labeled by letters in which each insurer has the same benefits.

So, the first step here is to determine the plan that best fits your coverage needs, but once you choose the best plan category, you know these coverages will be the same across all the different carriers – similar to an ice cream shop, chocolate is chocolate whether you go to Baskin Robbins or Cold Stone. In Medicare, Plan G is Plan G, whether through Humana or United Health Care. Based on this, once you find the plan for you, you can really shop by price and the carrier you prefer.

Last, we have part D, which covers prescription drugs and comes with an additional cost. Depending on the Medicare plan you choose, you will have a clear picture of what your premiums may look like. But what about the shared costs associated with significant health conditions?

Later in life the unfortunate likelihood of cancer, heart problems, and even the general costs of maintenance for our bodies goes up dramatically. As we get older, our health deteriorates, and it becomes more likely we will run into considerable health conditions. Caring for these conditions is not cheap. Luckily, insurance will help, but you should be prepared to come out of pocket for a portion of these costs as well.

Long Term Care

Many folks think of healthcare and long-term care as the same thing. They may believe that *long-term care* costs are even covered by Medicare. This is not the case, and in-fact, LTC is an entirely separate medical cost that is tied to "daily living" activities (feeding,

Activities of Daily Living (or ADLs) refer to the ability in bathing, eating, toileting, dressing, continence, and transferring.

bathing, etc.) and generally will not be covered by Medicare or standard health insurance.

> *My grandma was diagnosed with Alzheimer's and dementia soon after graduating from college. I have seen first-hand how tricky this can be. As with most from her generation, she could be a bit stubborn. 😊 She refused to take any professional help or go to a home. So, to help, my dad had to quit his job to take care of her full time. Unfortunately, this led to a lot of stress and challenges for him that eventually led to his passing when I was in my 20s. Illnesses like this have a major financial impact and a significant effect on the family and loved ones who are near to those who become sick.*

Long-term care expenses are typically the most concerning because of the cost required to provide for this care. The national average for full-time long-term care costs is roughly $80,000/year[*]. Add to that the taxes you may need to pay to take out of your account and your spouse's expenses still at home, and you can see how quickly things can go sideways.

Although you may have heard of long-term care *insurance* as the traditional way to prepare, there are other ways to cover these expenses that may not include insurance premiums. The most

*Source: https://longtermcare.acl.gov/costs-how-to-pay/costs-of-care.html

common misconception with long-term care is that Medicare or our health care will pay for these costs.

As previously stated, it will not, and it's important to account for this. There are state **Medicaid** programs designed to help with these costs, but to qualify for Medicaid you must have very little in assets. So, what are our options to prepare in today's world of high long-term care costs?

> Medicaid is a state sponsored insurance program that will provide long term care services for those who cannot afford the costs.

If you prefer to preserve your assets or cannot afford a long-term care event, insurance can be a great solution, but insurance is expensive. Our primary target for our clients is to save to a point where we can predict excess assets after providing for your retirement goals, allowing you to self-insure, by creating the ability to pay for these expenses through your assets directly.

Then, if we can self-insure, we start exploring tax efficiency opportunities to minimize this impact even further. For instance, if we were to *do the math*, and find that after funding all of your lifestyle goals you may still have assets at your passing, this additional buffer may provide enough excess to cover these expenses. In this scenario, we may explore **HSA** or Roth options to help provide a tax-free asset for this excess as well.

Of course, medical-related expenses are not the only consideration when we talk about the unexpected. The need to replace a roof, make home improvements or car repairs are all surface-level examples of where you may find large expenses come up out of the blue.

Taxes

Easily the largest and possibly one of the most misunderstood and missed expenses we face in our lifetime are taxes. Most don't even think of taxes as an expense, but that is what they are at the end of the day. If you aren't preparing to minimize this expense in your retirement, you are missing a huge planning opportunity. If we don't have flexibility in our tax planning, a change in tax laws or a significant tax bill can significantly impact your planning success.

We will go into tax planning in much greater detail. However, many folks also set themselves up for a significant tax bill without much thought to unexpected expenses in retirement when things do not go according to plan.

I shared earlier a story about a client's father who had followed the general rules of savings but did not take a personal approach to their planning. You may remember that their family ran into significant health costs that added up to about $9,000/month and a devastating impact on their financial abilities. They lost all of their resources quickly because they had to pull more money out than expected, and about half of their assets went to taxes simply because of the nature of the accounts. I have seen this time and time again, but it can all be avoided with some personal and thoughtful planning in place.

Loss of Income

We also need to put some thought into a loss of job or income. Everything you do, all of your plan – especially in your early years – hinges on your income to drive the machine. I can even understand the argument stating that your income-earning ability is by far your biggest asset, and therefore your biggest risk while growing your career may be a loss of income.

What if your income decreases or something were to happen where you lose this key driver? It's important to develop strategies as soon as possible to protect yourself from this major risk, and soon your plan may become bulletproof. Early on, it may be in the form of additional savings or disability insurance coverages to protect this income.

As your assets grow over time, ideally, you can get yourself to a point where your assets would be able to protect you in a period of lost income, this is what we would consider self-insuring, and creates a true example of your money working for you. This is an area where a taxable account (non-retirement) may help allow for more freedom.

More often, we hear about the impact of lost income in the event of our partner passing away. In this case, we may explore life insurance to protect us if a spouse were to pass away prematurely. Life insurance may not always the best answer but can play a role especially early on in our working lives. Early on, when we are starting to save, this loss may have a significant impact and life insurance may provide a large benefit for a small cost to get you back on your feet during a tough time. As you accumulate more, and especially as you move into retirement, we typically find life insurance becomes much less helpful.

Moral of the story, prepare for unexpected expenses, and always aim high in your savings target. You never know when they will come but they will show up. Life is expensive. Most people are one major medical issue, lawsuit, or home repair away from being broke. Be prepared, allow flexibility, and cushion in your planning.

VI. Risk Management

Whether you consider yourself a risk-taker or not, preserving your assets is critical. If you are starting to save, gearing up for retirement, or have accumulated enough wealth not to worry, managing risk is so important. All recent rhetoric says to buy the S&P 500 and let it go. Warren Buffet even says to buy an index fund, but if we look at his actions, he actually buys strong assets at a good value and will cut his losses when he has made a bad decision. So why don't people pay attention to what he actually does rather than what he says? Especially for a retiree in today's world, managing risk can be the difference between success and failure.

As humans, our wiring doesn't allow us to see risks for what they really are. We naturally downplay inherent risks to ourselves and tend to feel immortal until something happens. When creating a plan, we want to start with the offense strategies, as we need to score to win the game. But a championship team isn't built without defense.

Once we have our offense in place and developed the best savings and investing strategy possible, we need to be sure nothing can come along and derail us. We need to be sure our defense is in place to be as financially "bulletproof" as possible. Mark Twain once said, "What gets us into trouble is not what we don't know. It's what we know for sure that just ain't so." Inherently, we underestimate personal risks in our plans, saying *that will never happen to me*. Don't fall into this trap. Setting rules and strategies to avoid pitfalls can be invaluable in staying on track towards your goals.

Wars and Battles

We can start with set objectives and rules to determine what and when to buy or sell. You can stick to your plan and choose not to follow the shiny objects or chase the markets. You need a long-term allocation and strategy based on your objectives, but it is critical to understand the different risks prevalent at different times in a market cycle.

When establishing and reviewing your portfolio, you should start with the war in mind. The war is creating and managing through retirement and the long-term goal. That said, battles occur every quarter, every year, and there are often risks in a particular battle that could cost you the war. It's critical to make slight adjustments to your portfolio over time to handle these battles or you may slowly bleed through these battles and find that one has cost you the entire war.

Addressing asset allocation alone without adjusting to the current markets and risks relevant at the time is like testing your temperature as the only test to determine your health. You may not have the flu, but there are so many other illnesses you may need to be concerned about.

Interest Rate Risk

Whether you are just starting to save, or you are already in retirement, we need to worry about the eroding implications of inflation. To manage inflation risk, we use investments. One of the first places we look for safer investments is bonds. Now, bonds don't come without risk either. Bonds present a specific type of risk called *interest rate risk*. When you buy a bond, you are purchasing an instrument of debt, just like when we take on debt as consumers for a home or car.

As investors, we can loan money to companies, municipalities, the federal government, etc. Generally, you may give an entity $1,000 for them to use your money for ten years, and they pay you back the $1,000 at the end of that period (as you will see illustrated in the next diagram). But you should expect something in return for loaning your money, so you are offered interest each year.

Let's assume this entity pays you 4% every year for this exchange. Where might this be helpful? A fixed, set, income source is ideal in retirement, and it's why you hear so much about changing our portfolio to more bonds in retirement. The idea is not only to minimize risk, but more importantly, to create INCOME. Now, let's fast forward a year, and let's assume the interest rates rise. That same entity is now paying 6% for the same bond. How would you feel holding the bond at 4%? Probably not so great since there is something bigger, faster, and stronger out there.

So, if you wanted to sell your 4% machine, would you get more or less for it than the $1,000? As you may be expecting, the answer is less. Someone can buy the new stronger machine at 6% for $1,000, so they certainly would not be willing to pay this amount for a 4% machine. This scenario is called an inverse relationship where, when interest rates rise, bond prices fall.

The same applies when interest rates drop, bond prices increase. If you own individual bonds, you may be able to avoid this risk by simply not selling (although you may miss out on opportunity costs if there is a stronger machine available). But, what if you own an ETF or mutual fund made up of bonds? These type of bond funds may be subject to this type of interest rate movement. You may have no control over the fluctuation. However, others that are invested in the same fund may sell emotionally, forcing the fund to sell assets they may not want to, and leaving you with a mess of a return to deal with.

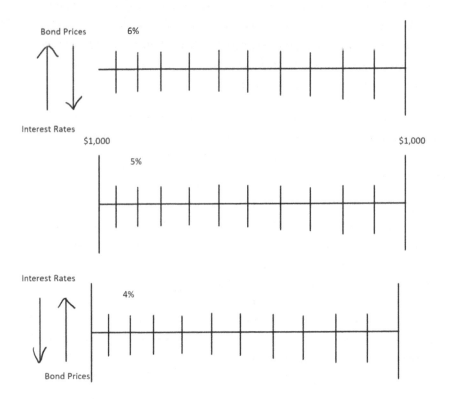

Credit Risk

Bonds also come with one of the most simple forms of risk: **credit risk**. When you loan money to an entity, their ability to pay you back is a risk you must understand. If you flip the scenario to consider yourself now as the borrower, you can understand credit risk from a more familiar scenario.

Let's say Joe is looking to get a line of credit or a mortgage. Now Joe has hopped around from job to job, he currently is on unemployment, and has a high amount of debt. Joe may still be able to get a loan, but what will Joe expect when he takes out this loan, he almost certainly can expect a higher interest rate as the "cost" of having bad credit.

On the flip side, let's say Jennifer is also looking for a mortgage. She has been with the same company for 15 years; she has a steady income and has no other debt. Her reward? She will most likely receive a better interest rate than Joe as a result of her good credit and history.

Like the individual, when you as an investor are loaning an entity money, one that has more risk of paying you back may need to make their borrowing parameters more attractive by paying a higher interest rate. Typically, the more risky the loan you are making, the higher the interest you may receive. Sometimes, these riskier bonds perform more like stocks (due to the interest rate risk we discussed above) and fluctuate quite a bit as compared to lower interest, lower risk bonds.

Market Risk

When we look for growth in our investments and make a move into stocks or equities, we begin to introduce **market risk**. Market risk may not be related to the stock or fund you choose specifically. Many times when the stock market as a whole drops in value, your funds may be affected as well even if the positions you own actually are not impacted by whatever function may be driving the market drop – this is market risk.

An index fund can be in the form of a Mutual Fund or ETF with a portfolio designed to mimic the performance of a particular index in one purchase. For better or worse, you will track each particular stock or holding within that index.

Especially these days in a world of general **index funds**, we find this to be the case more and more. This also opens opportunities when prices fluctuate for great stocks because everyone is simply buying the index and the more this becomes reality, the more opportunities you may find by taking the time to look.

Liquidity Risk

We previously discussed alternatives as another consideration in investing, allowing even further diversification above and beyond the traditional stock and bond portfolio. The concern with these types of investments is *liquidity risk*, or the inability to sell your assets in a timely manner. If you own gold bars, you may not be able to sell these quickly or may have to take a significant cut in the price to sell quickly if needed for an emergency.

Maybe a better example, if you own a Picasso painting and run into an emergency where you need the money quickly, you certainly should be able to sell that painting but may have to take a huge price cut in order to move quickly. The same applies to real estate and being unable to take out a chunk of the home for liquidity purposes, but all of these alternative assets provide great diversification properties when paired with stocks and bonds.

Risk is always a critical piece to address, and different risks may be more relevant at different times. As mentioned before, especially as you get closer to retirement or start taking distributions, market risk becomes a key driver to your plan's success. A loss of money is important.

Remember, as we covered earlier, when you lose 50% of your portfolio, what return you need to get back to even? You would need a 100% return from there just to get back to the same asset level you started with. So be careful listening to common advice about only worrying about averages. Long term focus is critical, but you need manage risk and minimize your downside in a bad year. Nobody will be immune to this but the less downside you take, the easier it is to climb out, and the better your "average" returns will look over time.

There was a family I had met with late in 2019 and early into 2020, let's call them Mr. and Mrs. Gekko. This family was retiring from a long career and was making the official transition to this next chapter of their lives first thing in 2020. They had always followed the general rules we hear repeatedly and had saved up a good chunk, but they were very hesitant about making any changes as they moved into retirement. They felt very confident in their ability to do it themselves with a very static investment approach.

I am sure we will not soon forget the events of 2020, as you very well know, come February 2020, we started hearing about this virus, COVID-19. Not too long after, COVID became the theme for the year. We saw our economy shut down and a huge, extremely fast drop in the stock market in March.

This family was far too aggressive at this stage and panicked when they saw the markets down near 40%, selling all of their assets to cash. We saw a rebound almost as quick as the drop in the markets, but by then, these folks were scarred. They refused to get back into the market based on what they saw in that February time-period. Even though they were not clients, I always strived to call them back within a few hours when they reached out. Hoping to help in any way that I could, I was also proactively reaching out to them.

Unfortunately, because these folks were unprepared and not willing to make changes ahead of time, they lost nearly half of their retirement assets in just one month. This experience resulted in concerns of getting back in, which led to a huge, missed run in the markets, leaving them with almost half of the assets they had just a few months ago. Now, they're left in a position where they need to make half the assets last just as long, almost certainly forcing them back to work or a reduced lifestyle.

When it comes to investing, there are three keys to managing your portfolio through market downturns:

1. BE PREPARED: You must have the pieces in place to handle these downturns BEFORE they come up, or you will find yourself making changes at a time that might hurt even more. You must start with truly detailed discussions about different scenarios you will face in the markets to ensure your allocation fits your comfort level.

If the Gekko family were to take the time with us to dig into the process and discuss risk, we would have found they were far too aggressive and worked towards a plan that included a more appropriate investment mix for them. We find far too often that investors are more aggressive than they really should be, whether by the allocation they set up or not understanding what is actually held in their Mutual Funds or ETFs.

This may lead to increased nerves through a market drop and possibly force you to sell at the worst time possible. I would suggest a third party to discuss your risk profile with to be sure a truly objective assessment is being made (could be a friend or trusted advisor).

2. MANAGE YOUR EMOTIONS: The hard work has been done ahead of time. Now one must manage emotions. It's challenging to play defense and take chips off the table when the markets are going up and up, but this is exactly what should be done.

The Gekko family did what most of us do as humans. They stuck their hand in the honey jar one too many times. If they were willing to give up just a little bit of upside in the early parts of 2020, their portfolio would have been in a better position to minimize the loss they saw in March significantly. Why is this so hard? The reason this is so difficult to do is because we are emotional creatures. As easy as it is to say this outside of the events, we cannot help to get euphoria when the markets are rising and absolute fear when they are dropping. As we are experiencing market growth, the key is to "take the chips off the table," allowing you to keep to your comfort zone. Taking chips off the table can be done in the form of rebalancing or even slight portfolio tweaks to a more strategic allocation based on the times.

Rebalancing is a very common strategy that keeps your investments in the allocation they were meant to be and, if done properly, would have saved this family their retirement. If you had a portfolio that was 50% stocks and 50% bonds, in a good year stock-wise, you may quickly find your portfolio is now 70% stocks and 30% bonds, leaving you in a much more risky position than you may want to be.

Rebalancing simply suggests you take the chips off the table, move back to your original 50/50 allocation, take money out of the stocks that have done well, and reinvest the proceeds into the bonds that may be on sale.

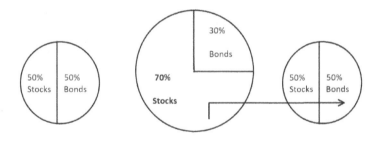

The most critical part is to be sure to do this while most people are wrapped up in the sugar high near the top, rather than struggling with the crash that follows the high. Instead, we find most individual investors getting more greedy, starting to have FOMO (fear of missing out) as the market gets frothy, and then getting nervous or selling when the market drops – creating the perfect storm of buying high and selling low (this is NOT the goal, we need to reverse this). This is what the Gekko's experienced and is all too common with individual investors during these marketing swings as emotions take over. Assume you were to buy a pen today for a dollar, the next day, there is a massive oversupply of pens for some reason, and that pen is now only worth 50 cents. Being the smart person you are, you know you are holding this pen for the long term and you hold this pen for three years to sell at $5 at that time. How much did you lose when the pen was worth 50 cents? None right? You actually experienced a gain of $4 because you stuck with it and maintained your long-term goals.

Now, how did you feel at these times? You probably felt a bit concerned when the pens were priced so low but after holding and selling at $5, you felt great. This is the challenge with market swings and how emotions can play a role in our investment decisions. If we can manage our emotions effectively, you can allow yourself to be a much better investor for the long term.

3. TAKE ADVANTAGE OF DIPS: Assuming you were able to handle steps 1 and 2 properly, now is the time to take advantage of these lower prices. It's funny, when we find a sale at our favorite retail shop, we can't resist but to take advantage of the sale. But, when the market or real estate prices are on sale, we shy away and get fearful thinking the world is coming to an end.

The Gekko family wasn't able to do so and actually went in the other direction, selling their assets while discounted. Of course, this is the worst thing we can do in these times. Instead, we should use this time to find the cash in the cushions and look for additional funds to put to work! It's impossible to time the bottom and please be careful of "catching a falling knife." Instead, by dollar cost averaging (set periodic investments) into the market during downturns, you can help to keep your emotions in check and set up a high likelihood of buying at a lower average price.

It's so easy to stand here coolheaded and think that this three-step process is simple to follow, but we are humans and can all become victims to the difficulties of market swings. The wealthy seem to have one major commonality; they do not lose money. That is because they understand the importance of severe negative returns and how difficult it can be to make up for large losses. Yet, the common advice for everyone is to weather the storm and not worry.

To truly make the most of your resources, take notes from the wealthy, don't give in to this advice and understand the importance in minimizing losses. Take control of your finances and add in risk control measures to reduce the downside as much as possible while still maintaining a long-term focus. Nobody is immune to losses. If the market drops your portfolio will no matter how well it is managed. However, if you take half the loss of the "market," you will be surprised how much easier it is to climb back up.

The world has changed; we can no longer simply set up a stock and bond portfolio and expect to manage risk appropriately. We are in a time where markets move quicker, and the old rules of investing have shown cracks. Today's world requires the use of these risk management strategies, not only to minimize risk in your investments but in your planning strategies and life planning to allow yourself as much flexibility as possible.

VII. Social Security

Social Security is so complicated and intricate that I could have easily written an entire book on this subject alone. There are around 80 different combinations to file for Social Security for a married couple at this time, so clearly, Social Security can be quite a complicated topic.

Social Security is a perfect example of a "guaranteed" income source (don't laugh), and a great vehicle to use to match up against your expense needs. For most, Social Security may not be enough to provide for all of your expenses, but it is still an important piece of retirement planning and should be viewed as another strategy to be sure to make the most of.

The History of Social Security

Social Security was initially established back in the mid-1930's as a result of the Great Depression. The program was enacted as a social program similar to what other developed civilizations had created. Far before Social Security, many groups and civilizations would create their own financial security together so that if one person in the group suffered financial hardship, the others would be able to chip in and help out.

Although Social Security has evolved a bit since it began, the program itself is generally pretty similar to its original structure. Back in the '30s, our lifespan was significantly shorter than what we experience today in 2020. The government did not originally create the program to handle someone in retirement for 30 years, and this is where a lot of the issues we face have come into play. That said, it is still a program available to U.S. workers and one that nearly all of us need to understand. Social Security began as a way to pay into a system so that you can accept a paycheck in your retirement years to supplement your income when you are no longer working.

<u>Qualifying for Social Security</u>

We pay into Social Security throughout our entire working years. So, many of us are anxious to get our benefits. One of the first questions that comes up is: *when do I qualify for benefits?* Before we get into qualifying, it's important to understand that Social Security is actually a suite of benefits that you buy into over time.

Most think of the retirement benefit, and that will be our focus for this reading, but Social Security also provides disability benefits, a small death benefit, etc. To qualify for Social Security retirement benefits, you must have 40 credits. Naturally, the next question is: *well, what the heck is a credit?* A credit is one-quarter of employment income. There is a very low minimum earnings test to qualify for a credit, but for this purpose, let's just assume that if you work for a quarter, you will receive one credit.

So, doing the math, if we work for ten years (four quarters per year), we would be eligible for Social Security benefits. It is also important to understand that there is a cap when it comes to Social Security benefits. If you make over a certain threshold in a given year, you actually will not notice any larger benefit based on the additional income over the threshold.

Regarding the retirement benefit, most of us have bought into the program after ten working years, but we can't start our retirement benefits until age 62. We can choose to start our benefits any time between the ages of 62 and 70, and most of our "**full retirement age**" will land at age 67. That doesn't mean you need to start benefits at 67. In fact, the longer you wait to start these benefits, the more you will receive monthly. We see many common themes when it comes to Social Security benefits. Many folks have been advised under the old model to take Social Security right away when they are eligible, or others try to take benefits right at full retirement age. The truth is, this is usually with little thought.

Strategy

The most common strategy we see is a calculation based on longevity and longevity alone. We bring value by helping keep away from emotional decisions and exploring all often-missed angles. This cookie-cutter version of Social Security planning suggests you can find the crossover point – as shown in the figure below - if you were to wait until age 70 (as you will get more monthly to do so) and determine if you may live longer than this break-even age.

As you might imagine, if you live longer and receive a higher monthly benefit, you can calculate a particular age that would show a higher lifetime benefit for every month you live past that point. If you base your analysis on this amount and do live a long life, you would be ahead, and if you passed away earlier, you would have left money on the table.

However, there is so much missing here. This is a great start to analyzing Social Security benefits, but much more needs to be addressed these days to really maximize this tool and to fit into the bigger picture as best it can. To get the most of your Social Security resources in today's world, sometimes it may mean taking benefits early, other times delaying benefits as long as possible. For married couples, often, it may even mean staggering benefits for each spouse to maximize your plan.

Age	Total Benefit Accrued	
	Age 62	Age 70
62	33276	
65	133104	
70	299484	48660
75	465864	291960
80	632244	535260
85	798624	778560
90	965004	1021860

The key around Social Security today is not merely to consider your options in a silo, but rather to explore how these choices may impact your other assets as a whole. Social Security is one tool in a vast retirement toolbox you will have available to you and, just like with everything else we have discussed, should not be looked at in a vacuum.

Using the right tool at the right time is what makes a great carpenter. It is critical to explore how to use this tool with the others to make the most of your retirement assets as a whole. The combination of Social Security and your other income streams will have an effect on taxation and even the amount you receive from Social Security, so don't take this at surface level.

Social Security Taxation

Did you catch that? Yes, believe it or not, Social Security benefits can be taxed. We often see retirees taking Social Security benefits only to later find the impacts of these benefits on their taxation. If you have provisional income (defined as half of your SS benefits and basically every other dollar you receive) above a certain threshold, 85% of your Social Security benefit would be taxed as ordinary income.

As of 2020, a married couple with a provisional income over $44,000 would be forced to pay income taxes on 85% of their Social Security benefits. If you find yourself between $32k and $44k, 50% of your benefit is taxed, and under $32k, there is no taxation on your benefits. So, keep this in mind as part of your Social Security analysis and any strategies you may be exploring during these prime planning years.

Married Filing Jointly	Single	Share of benefit that is taxed
0-$32k	0-$25k	0%
$32-$44k	$25-$34k	50%
Above $44k	Above $34k	85%

Withheld Social Security Benefits

Not only can Social Security be taxed, but if you are working while receiving benefits, the Social Security Administration may also withhold some of your payments. Many retirees concerned about Social Security's viability may be inclined to take these benefits as soon as possible but be aware of these hidden impacts.

Taking Social Security benefits before your "full retirement age" may lead to withheld benefits. If you are working during the years before full retirement, and make above a quite minimal income, half of your Social Security benefit will be held back. Now, I use the term "held back" on purpose because these benefits will be paid back to you at full retirement age, but if your goal was to take money out as soon as possible, you might not even be getting the full benefit you deserve in this scenario. I pose the question: *do you want to pay into something for 30 years and turn on the faucet only to find out that half of your benefits won't even be paid out to you?*

What about the connection between Social Security and Medicare? These are two completely different programs, but believe it or not, your Social Security choices will have some impacts on your Medicare benefits. The first factor is the easiest, which is how premiums will be paid. In short, any Medicare premiums are taken out of Social Security benefits if you are receiving them.

However, if you have elected to delay your Social Security payments, the Medicare premiums may need to be paid out of your bank like any other cost. Second, and perhaps more important, is understanding that your Medicare premiums are actually based on your income. We talked a bit ago about how Social Security benefits may be taxed. Additionally, suppose you make above a certain amount annually. In that case, your Medicare premiums may be tied to your income, and you may see your Medicare premiums increase as a result of your benefit election and other income sources.

So, there is clearly a lot to consider as social security stands today, but what about the future of Social Security? Will it be around throughout my retirement? Will it be in the same form or some Social Security 2.0? This has been a concern on savers minds for decades now.

For those reading this near 2020, the city of Detroit bankruptcy may still be fresh enough in your memory to know how difficult this was to many city workers. Many retirees had worked for the city their whole life, they based all of their retirement planning around the "guarantee" that the city was going to pay them these pension benefits and they felt a false sense of security that the city was going to take care of them.

As you know, the story didn't end so happy for those retirees. The city declared bankruptcy in 2015, and those pensions were now paying pennies on the dollar. Retirees across the city had little hope and a much less exciting lifestyle in their retirement. The takeaway here, guarantees are only as strong as the entity backing those guarantees. So, even with an entity as strong as the US government, just be aware things can change. The government has shown time and time again they will make changes and some that have major effects on our lives as citizens, so do you want to rely on the stability in a program like this that is already underfunded?

I don't believe Social Security will completely disappear, but I do think something needs to change. For those closer to retirement, I believe it would be tough for the government to make much change to the benefits you have been relying on your whole life. For those further out, it has to change. We will most likely see later ages to begin benefits, rather than eligibility between ages 62-70.

Maybe eligibility becomes tiered based on age groups so those further away from retirement may have to wait until later ages to begin claiming benefits. Or we may see much smaller benefit amounts, perhaps they will cut benefits down from the current projections to take pressure off the Social Security fund. Wherever you are on this spectrum, I would encourage you to consider if you want to leave your retirement prospects subject solely to a federal program that is already failing.

Social Security is tricky nowadays. Not only do we have to consider how best to use this tool as a part of our overall plan, we also have to consider how much of this to rely on in our assumptions. If you have the luxury to do so, consider ways to make this as small a part of your plan as possible. If you are closer to retirement (and benefits may not be changed on you) and you are relying on this, consider these strategies to be sure you get the most out of a system you have been paying over 12% of your income into your whole life. Just like we take decisions around our 401(k)s and pensions very deliberately, after paying into the Social Security program for so long, our choices with these benefits should require the same level of attention and should evolve as the world changes.

VIII. Tax Planning

Tax planning is an area I feel is most often overlooked and can truly make the biggest difference given all the tools we have available as investors these days. There are rules of thumb everywhere you turn to address tax planning. But with some real thought and strategy in place, you can be sure you aren't paying more in taxes than you should be over your lifetime.

It's essential to understand the tax impacts of EVERY change you make on short term and long-term plans. Every single decision we make throughout a year will have tax impacts. The crazy thing is that the advice we hear overlooks tax strategies, only reviewing them once a year (typically when filing taxes for that year) which could be losing you money. I understand taxes are not the most exciting topic, but this area has become more and more important as the tax code continues to evolve and become more complicated.

Those who see the value in thoughtful tax planning can take back more direct control and allow more freedom if appropriately addressed. Proper tax planning is 100% in your control and can help to minimize "drag" on your planning, allowing you to keep as much of your hard-earned money as possible.

Why do we invest? Do we invest simply to get by or invest for the opportunity of a better future? This is important to consider when it comes to tax planning and challenging the common tax planning rhetoric. Paying more in income taxes during your working years may not be your problem. The more income we earn or savings we accumulate, often the more we pay in taxes. This doesn't need to be the case.

The wealthy use investments that create flexibility and improve their situation by creating more tax-efficient strategies for the future rather than paying income taxes on their employment income and retirement income their WHOLE LIFE. These tools are not just for the wealthy. With proper planning and thoughtful strategies, you can create tax efficiencies for your future too.

Earlier, we laid out the three broad ways your investments can be taxed. The key is not to have one-third of your assets in each bucket but to be better prepared for the future by diversifying your tax implications, just like you would the investments within these accounts.

Just in 2020, the passing of the **SECURE Act** is a great example of how quickly tax laws can change and by having assets in each bucket, it will allow you to be as nimble as you can be. This will allow you to minimize the overall tax impacts over your life and your legacy by pulling from the right assets at the right time.

In the beginning of 2020 new legislation was passed called the *SECURE Act*. There were many provisions, but the biggest change was to the requirements around distributions with inherited retirement accounts.

Prior to the change, the beneficiary was required to take distributions based on their life. After the changes, a beneficiary must deplete the entire account within ten years.

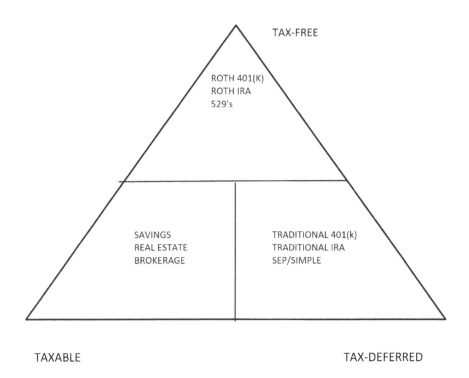

TAX-FREE

ROTH 401(K)
ROTH IRA
529's

SAVINGS
REAL ESTATE
BROKERAGE

TRADITIONAL 401(k)
TRADITIONAL IRA
SEP/SIMPLE

TAXABLE   TAX-DEFERRED

Tax-Deferred

You may have been investing under the general rule of thumb that you should always invest in the traditional, pre-tax side of your retirement accounts. This advice indicates you are earning more income during your working years and therefore paying more in taxes today than you will be in retirement so deferring those taxes is going to be better. If you are a high earner and in a high tax bracket, tax deductions are important and something we aim to help us as much as possible during those high earning years. At first glance, this all seems very reasonable. But, is this the best option for your future and your goal with investing?

Many who have followed this advice find they have set up a ticking time bomb, paying more in taxes in retirement than they were in their working years. *This especially penalizes those who are excellent savers.* Maybe you will have less income in retirement; maybe you won't. What do you really want your retirement to look like? Would you like to downsize your lifestyle in retirement? If so, this may work. But for those who want to set themselves up to enjoy even more freedom in retirement, there may be more strategic solutions. Rather than the cookie-cutter view addressing your taxes today, proper planning should address your future and minimize your lifetime tax bill not just the bill this year.

Something else missing in this assumption is future tax rates. Currently, in 2020, tax rates are the lowest they have ever been. With the government's spending habits and especially all the spending we see during this year of the COVID pandemic, we will likely see taxes increase in the future to make up for these deficits. In fact, in a few years, the current lower tax brackets are set to expire and bounce back to the pre-tax cuts rates already (and very possible we see even further increases from here). In this scenario, as you might imagine, those willing to "bite the bullet" and pay taxes today to create tax-free assets for the future may be much better off.

> The Federal budget has been running at a deficit for a very long time. The debt has become significant and many feel taxes may increase to help the government begin to pay down this debt.

I sat down with a new client earlier this year who had done a great job of savings. They were in their early 50s and had managed to put aside just over $2M in retirement assets. As a Boeing engineer, she was making a respectable income. Given the earnings over her life, it was very clear she was a major saver and had done a great job of keeping disciplined, building her future nest egg. The challenge was that every single dollar of her over $2M in assets was saved to the pre-tax 401(k). Now we may all sit here and say, so what, they saved a great amount and may be comfortable, but I challenge you to consider what the impact may be.

How can we improve this client's situation? As someone in her early 50s, the restrictions in a pretax vehicle have held her back from considering an "early" retirement. (As you may be aware, we cannot access our pre-tax 401(k)s or IRAs until age 59½ without penalties associated with early distributions.) Now, there are some ways around this, such as Section 72(t) which may be a bit beyond the purpose of this text, but they can limit our flexibility in the future. However, if the client had repositioned some assets in a Roth IRA or NQ account, she could retire today without many negative long-term impacts. Second, the future RMDs for this client, and her lifetime taxation was going to be massive!

Because she was okay with working longer, we were able to address this and outlined a plan to reposition some existing assets and contribute new monies into more tax-efficient vehicles, creating a total tax savings over her lifetime that equals nearly half of her total assets!

Required Minimum Distributions (RMDs)

The required minimum distributions, or RMDs, I mentioned are very often overlooked. At age 72, the IRS will force you to take money out of your pre-tax or traditional retirement accounts (IRAs, 401(k)s, etc.) every single year, called a *required minimum distribution*. Because you have not paid a penny in taxes on these accounts throughout their existence, the IRS wants what is coming to them. They have created a way to ensure they receive these taxes by requiring you to take distributions from these retirement accounts.

Not only must you take these funds out of your account, but the distribution is also fully taxable as ordinary income. Suppose much of your life savings is in these vehicles. In that case, you may find this distribution to be quite impactful, throwing off your income plans, and maybe even bumping you up tax brackets or negatively affecting your Medicare and Social Security benefits. If you find yourself in a position where these RMDs are more than you need, another strategy to consider is even delaying your Social Security benefits to take money out of your pre-tax assets early on.

By delaying your social security income, you both deplete your pre-tax asset base for future RMDs – lowering the amount you would be required to take from your accounts. Additionally, this will keep your taxation as minimal as possible throughout your distribution years, minimizing taxes on Social Security. There is a lot to explore under these circumstances, but often, this can be a great tax planning strategy.

Age	Investor A RMD - $1M Pre-Tax IRA	Investor B RMD - $1M Roth IRA
72	$ 39,062.52	0
73	$ 40,485.83	0
74	$ 42,016.81	0
75	$ 43,668.12	0
76	$ 45,454.55	0
77	$ 47,169.81	0
78	$ 49,261.08	0
79	$ 51,282.05	0
80	$ 53,475.94	0

So, how can we use these different tax buckets to create more freedom? We may want to explore diversifying our taxes in these different categories. Consider the retirement you want to create, your situation today, risks you may encounter along the way, and establish strategies in each category that will allow you to make the most of these categories.

Tax-Free

The second-place savers typically look is the Roth or tax-free bucket. The great thing about the Roth bucket is

Fun Fact! The Roth 401(k) does still require a retiree to take distributions under the RMDs. There is a simple fix, by rolling over these assets into your own Roth IRA, the required distributions no longer apply.

the distributions and growth from this bucket are completely tax-free.

In addition, these assets are immune to the RMD challenges I had shared above. Roth IRAs also have a special rule that allows access to these funds before the traditional "retirement age" of 59 ½ years old. With Roth IRAs, once an account has been opened and funded for five years, you actually have the freedom to access the basis, or contribution, part of your account tax and penalty-free. For instance, let's say the client we discussed were to contribute $250k into a Roth over several years and that account grew to be worth a total of $1M. She would not be able to access the full balance without penalty before retirement age but would be able to access the $250k in contributions without penalties. This would allow $250k of assets to help bridge the gap until 59 ½.

Now, the purpose of this account should be earmarked for retirement, but this nuance can provide a lot of flexibility against the unexpected and also allow for an "early" retirement if desired. Remember, the Roth's biggest benefit is that every dollar in this account is 100% tax-free forever, as long as it is used for qualified distributions. This is huge!

Let's say that five years from now the government revamps the tax code and sets up huge tax hikes. No problem since your assets are tax-free. What if the Social Security tax or Medicare tax is increased? Again, no problem since your assets are tax-free. Keep in mind that it is very likely most of your assets in retirement will be from growth in your account, not contributions. The whole point of investing is for those dollars to grow.

Let's look at an example where the initial $1,000 you invest grows to $10,000 by the time you need to take distributions. Would you rather pay taxes on the $1,000 initial contribution or the $10,000 harvest in the future?

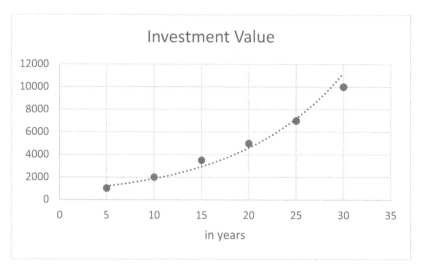

Investment Value

This is a hypothetical example and is for illustrative purposes only. No specific investments were used in this example.

Although there is more to this concept, you see how powerful tax-free assets can be for your future!

<u>Taxable</u>

One of the most often overlooked and underutilized buckets are taxable assets. Most are familiar with pre-tax and tax-free accounts, but many of us focus on savings in these retirement buckets, altogether leaving out the taxable buckets. Taxable accounts do not receive deferral benefits, and instead, you are taxed as you go. You may pay taxes on any income you receive from a particular investment or you may experience taxation for selling an investment at a gain.

For example, if you were to buy XYZ stock at $100 and sell it at $250, you would be taxed at capital gains rates in the year you sold the stock on the $150 of gains. Capital gains rates are different from income tax rates and can get a bit tricky, but the most simple way to understand these taxes is based on the holding period. As long as you were to buy and hold a position for one year or more, the gains would be taxed at a long-term gains rate, which is a flat 15% (20% if you are in the top tax bracket). Using the example above, if you purchased XYZ stock at $100 on 4/14/2019 and sold it for $250 any time after 4/14/2020, you may be taxed 15% of the $150 gain, resulting in a tax of $22.50.

If you were to sell an investment within less than a year of the purchase date, you may be subject to short term gain tax rates, which would be considered the same as ordinary income and taxed accordingly. If you sold that same XYZ stock at $250 before 4/14/2020 (less than one year), the $150 would be added to your income for the year and taxed at the rate based on your income tax bracket.

Outside of the tax considerations, these accounts can provide a really important aspect to our strategies allowing for flexibility – unlimited contribution amounts, no age requirements for money in or out, or income limits to utilize these vehicles.

Now, taxable accounts do not come without downsides. The challenges with these accounts are. of course, we pay taxes as we go. When you do experience tax implications, this tax must be paid as opposed to keeping that tax deferred. This allows you to reinvest all of these dollars back into the account, which is the case with the other two buckets.

Within these taxable accounts, nuanced tax strategies become really important as well. For instance, you may consider using **municipal bonds** for your income exposure, allowing you to receive interest federally tax-free.

For municipal bonds, you may need to pay state income taxes on the income. Depending on your state and income tax policies (or not), it may help dictate your holdings.

Another extremely impactful strategy is what is called **tax-loss harvesting**. This strategy allows you to sell a stock or position at a loss and simultaneously buy a similar position. The strategy maintains your portfolio composition but gives you the ability to recognize a tax "loss" for the year that can either offset other gains, earned income, or be carried forward to future years.

> Municipal bonds are debt instruments issued by municipalities, such as for schools or road repairs. The interest you receive on these bonds are exempt from federal income tax but may still be subject to state income tax if you are in a state with a local tax.

Consider how these different vehicles may relate to the unexpected expenses and risk management challenges I keep referring to. The Roth and taxable buckets create a lot of flexibility to minimize your tax impacts when a large distribution is needed to fund an emergency. If all of your assets are in a pre-tax vehicle, you may experience a huge hit to take funds to pay for these expenses. If you are before retirement age, you may not even be able to handle it out of the tax-deferred vehicle without penalties.

Although we may not want to set up our plan solely to benefit the next generation or the ones we love, some proper steps in our own planning may also lead to a more impactful legacy for our heirs. Estate planning is exceptionally personal and complicated (more to come on this topic), but the Roth family of accounts can be a considerable tool in tax planning for your family.

Roth IRAs do not require RMDs and any amount your heirs receive is also 100% income tax-free to them, allowing the freedom to use as needed and allowing the asset the ability to grow for a long time with fully tax-free growth benefits. During the craziness of 2020, we saw other legislation pass that really impacted the pre-tax assets. I think one of the biggest take-aways from these changes is that when we have assets that are tax-free, changes in policy and taxes may not affect us as much.

> Remember the SECURE Act? This change had a significant impact on those with pre-tax assets. The change not only forced account holders to deplete the entire balance within ten years but also pay the taxes on the distributions as well.

Strategy

If you have done a good job in tax planning, another important consideration comes up, which is determining which assets to spend down first. The old approach was to defer taxes as long as you can, even as you move into a distribution mode. This can make sense, but what if legacy is important to you and you find you were simply deferring taxes to create a larger bill for your heirs? It doesn't mean that was wrong, but a new approach may help you find strategies that help you based on your priorities.

You may also want to consider the impact of RMDs to you. We often find RMDs are projected to be more than our clients need, and by delaying taxes, we are simply creating a bigger tax bill for future years. It may be helpful for those in this position to actually take out your tax-deferred assets first, followed by Roth, and ending with taxable assets.

This may be able to help minimize your future RMDs, create a larger tax-free bucket to use later in life for major medical costs, and leave taxable assets to your heirs as they may receive a *"step-up in basis"*. This means that they could actually consider their cost basis on a particular stock based on the value the date they receive the funds from inheritance. This basically wipes out large tax bills from any significant gains that might have been incurred if you sold it during your lifetime. The point is that it's not a one-size-fits-all.

> Step up in basis refers to a particular tax strategy. When an heir inherits an asset, the new cost basis in that particular asset can be based upon the value at the date of death. This helps the heir to minimize potential large taxes on gains.

As discussed in our expenses chapters, we would all love to plan for the perfect retirement where everything goes according to plan. The reality, this NEVER happens. When planning a road trip, it is wise to plan ahead for potential issues you might face (blown tires or unexpected stops), but many miss this step in retirement planning. What if things don't go according to plan and you run into that blown tire along the way?

If the only funds available are in a pre-tax assets, not only will these changes lead to a larger decrease in your portfolio, but they can increase your tax bill. This also could increase the taxation on your Social Security benefits and the costs for your Medicare premiums. A plan built around all pre-tax assets may work well if we knew exactly how much we need each year and that the tax implication of these distributions are low. But life, taxes, and the unexpected can change this picture very quickly.

The key to effective tax planning is to allow for flexibility in the future to adjust as needed. Although these tools are helpful now, proper planning is never stagnant due to legislation and tax law changes, so be prepared to adjust as needed to maximize any changes that are thrown your way. You now have clarity on where and why tax planning can become so important, now use the strategies outlined in these chapters to maximize your plan and minimize your tax implications.

The old approach seems to take a lackadaisical view on the tax planning side of things, but taxes are almost always an individual's biggest expense, and we can avoid this mistake. With a proper, more modern approach to planning, you can take back control and set yourself up to be in a position where you are not constantly working or investing to the benefit of the IRS.

IX.   Estate Planning Basics

Let's start with the most crucial question around estate planning: *who needs to worry about it?* The short answer is EVERYONE. A common misconception is that only those with significant assets and tax concerns need to address estate planning. These days, however, whether you are 20 years old with an Xbox as your only asset or a retiree with significant assets, everyone needs some level of estate planning.

As you might imagine, the 20-year-old's estate plan may not need to be nearly as complex as the retirees, but both should have some thought to their estate. If you find yourself in a similar position to the 20-year-old, it may be as simple as defining who would receive that Xbox of yours if something were to happen to you. For those with significant assets, your planning may include trusts, gifting, and more complicated strategies to enhance and preserve your estate. But, either way, you will need to understand the basics and put some thought into mapping out your goals.

When I ask my clients about their legacy wishes, some have clear intentions of what they would like to establish and how they would like to be remembered. Other times, when I am working with folks who have little excess, the initial response is to say that this is not important to them. Often, when I dig deeper to get to their true wishes, I find they really do care. They are just concerned with their own well-being and they are not sure they would be able to make any legacy wishes come true without negatively impacting their own retirement abilities. Proper estate planning can be such a useful tool for tackling legacy concerns on either end of the spectrum, bringing strategies to the table that will help both save taxes and allow for legacy wishes.

Although most think of estate planning as what may be left to heirs when they leave this earth, something else to consider is that your legacy is not just transferred assets. Your legacy can also be what you do and the impact you make while living. This can come in many forms, whether helping with education funding for family, philanthropic interests, life lessons or memories with loved ones, or simple gifting strategies to those you care about most. The key is, legacy planning is extremely personal. With some real thought, it's possible your wishes will be carried out no matter the circumstances.

How Assets Pass

When discussing leaving money to heirs, there are a few ways assets can pass. The first is **by law**; this would include titling on accounts, joint tenancy, etc. If you have a bank account titled as, "Joint tenants with rights of survivorship" with your spouse, the law dictates that the joint tenant on the account would automatically assume the account at your passing.

The second is by contract. This is the most common form we see. If you have a retirement account or any insurance in place you most likely have named a beneficiary, this is **by contract**. The contract you have set up for this particular account names a specific person or entity who would receive your assets when you pass.

The third is **by will**, and this is for the rest of your belongings. A will ensures assets that are not addressed with beneficiary designations or set up under law will go to the person of your choosing.

Last, is by state laws of intestacy (or **probate**). This is NOT desired. If you have ever dealt with probate directly, you understand how painful and long this process can be. Each state has a set plan for your assets, and in lieu of any or all of the items above, the state ultimately decides where assets will be passed. Now they don't pick someone at random. They have a defined "pecking order" based on relationships. However, this defined order may not always go where you intend.

Probate

Any time we bring in state governments, attorneys, and courts, you might imagine this adds A LOT of time to the equation. So, we do not want to strive towards a plan that passes through probate. Rather, by setting up the proper documents and beneficiary designations, we can help minimize this process as much as possible. Now, assets passing through a will still go through probate, but these wishes generally help to ensure things go as smoothly as possible.

Often, the situation occurs where a beneficiary on a retirement account is listed, but the will states another person to receive the assets. Generally speaking, the beneficiary or legal designations will trump the will in this scenario. The fact that beneficiaries are our first line of defense shows why reviewing beneficiaries can be so important to be sure there is no discrepancy.

This also underscores the importance of updating wills. You may expect it would be a good idea to update wills in the event of major life shifts; kids, marriages, divorces, etc. But, I would also suggest time is a factor in this equation too. Over time, you may have accumulated other assets that are not listed in your will or state laws may have changed. It can be critical to update these documents regularly, whether life shifts have occurred or not.

My father passed away when I was in my late 20s. It was an extremely tough time for me to lose my father, and at such a young age. My father didn't have a lot of assets by any means, and this typically makes estate planning a bit easier. Even with only personal belongings in his estate, I found myself only three days after his passing watching my family argue over a Keurig Coffee Machine. They were at each other's throats about who it belongs to... a Keurig Coffee Machine! This was so soon into his passing it amazed me.

I know everyone deals with death differently, but while I was grieving my father's passing, this was the last thing I wanted to hear. Unfortunately, a family member's passing can bring out the worst in people and shows how important it can be to have a very thought-out estate planning in place to minimize this added stress and contention between family members.

Beneficiary Designations

A straightforward and important step in proper estate planning is to be sure to review and update beneficiaries regularly. All of your retirement accounts, life insurance policies, or transfer on death assets (whether through your employer or personal accounts) have beneficiary designations. Unfortunately, I can't even count the number of times I have seen the beneficiary designations still listed as a spouse from a prior marriage. (Or even multiple marriages ago!)

Beneficiary designations are a contractual agreement, so a widow attempting to receive the benefits intended for them when a beneficiary arrangement says otherwise is extremely challenging. Almost always, the individual listed as the beneficiary will receive the assets. Passing away with outdated beneficiaries can cause a whole list of issues for family members, so please make it a regular priority to review your beneficiaries and make updates as needed.

The common old school approach to estate planning outlines a simple beneficiary check. This is important, but there are a few other key documents nearly everyone needs in these times. If you find you are in a more complex scenario (such as having significant assets saved, a complex family dynamic, or have assets in other states or countries), then you may want to consider additional strategies. We will touch on some of these later on in this chapter. A few documents are key at the basic level, including a last will and testament, a power of attorney, health care directives, and a living will.

Last Will and Testament

Most may be familiar with a **last will and testament**. This is one of the most common estate planning documents, designed to dictate who gets your belongings when you pass. The key to remember is that account titling and beneficiaries are typically going to trump the will, but this can catch the rest of things that do not have beneficiary designations in place (such as coffee machines). Even a very well-written will needs to go through probate but having a will in place can help to expedite this tedious process.

Although a living will may sound the same, it is quite different. A living will is your "try twice and let me go orders." A more P.C. version is the *do not resuscitate* orders. Especially if you have strong feelings towards this or are worried about your family's expenses for continued health care, a living will is critical.

Power of Attorney (POA)

Power of attorney, or POA, is another critical document. A POA specifies a person that can make choices on your behalf. A power of attorney can be set up for financial, health, or all-encompassing decisions. It can be imperative if something were to happen to you, medically or your mental ability were to decline at some point. A **healthcare directive** is a specific form of power of attorney that allows you to name someone other than your power of attorney, specifically for healthcare decisions. The reason we may sometimes suggest a separate designee may be based on proximity. These days, having someone across the country to help with financial decisions may work just fine, but what happens if that person is forced with a difficult medical decision to make on your behalf? Someone nearby may be extremely valuable in this scenario so that they can assess the situation in its entirety and consult with medical professionals. Something else that has become more relevant recently is a healthcare directive on adult children.

Let's use a client story; we'll call him Mr. Joe. Mr. Joe's kid was starting college and unfortunately was part of a tragic accident where he was knocked unconscious while at university. Mr. Joe was notified and went to the hospital to help. Since his son was over 18 years old, it created a world of headaches to take care of his son. This could have been avoided with a healthcare directive, allowing him to make decisions and receive medical information for his son.

Estate Taxes

When considering estate planning documents, it is critical to understand that your estate is calculated based on ALL of your assets accumulated over your lifetime. When you pass away, your estate includes everything from cash to real estate and even life insurance benefits. It is important to have this understanding as a baseline to work through any level of estate planning strategies.

For those who have a significant estate, we need to touch on a key area when we discuss estate planning, which is the impact of estate taxes, or death taxes/inheritance taxes. If your estate is over a certain threshold, there can be very steep tax associated with every dollar above that amount, and they can be due very quickly. Not only is there a federal estate tax exemption limit, but certain states also have their own limits before taxation comes into play. As we move into more advanced estate planning strategies, these concepts can get quite dense. In the next few paragraphs, we will take some time to dig into these complexities on a high level to introduce considerations for those with a significant estate to consider.

At either the federal or the state levels, these exemption limits are subject to change. In 2020, the federal estate tax exemption is quite high historically (right around $11.5M). Not too long ago, it was closer to $1M. So, even if you find yourself below these limits today, it doesn't mean you can leave this consideration out of the picture. You may want to keep an eye on it and continue to adjust as needed. Here in my home state of Washington, we also have a significantly lower state estate tax exemption at near $2.5M. This means that if your home, investments, retirement, life insurance, and everything were valued at over $2.5M when you pass, your estate would need to pay taxes on the assets above that threshold. It can be critical to understand these exemptions and have flexibility in your plan if these levels change or you move to a state that has laws your previous home state did not.

<u>Gifting</u>

If you find you are above these exemptions, you can minimize this impact by giving away assets earlier to decrease your estate below these levels. Such a strategy can be very effective in creating the same impact to your heirs with a much smaller tax implication.

At the federal level, it is helpful to know that there is a gifting limit. The first consideration is that there is an annual gifting limit ($15k in 2020) where everything below this amount slips under the radar and does not affect any other limits. Any gifts above that will start to decrease your lifetime gifting exclusion. At this time, the estate tax exemption and the lifetime gift exemption are the same amounts and work in lockstep at the federal level.

As an example, if the estate tax exemption is $11.5M and you decided to give away $1,015,000 in any given year, the first 15k would be a non-event. However, the remaining $1M gift would actually decrease your gifting exemption which is later taken from your estate exemption by that same amount. This means that if you passed away after this gift, your estate tax exemption would now be $10.5M as opposed to the original $11.5M amount. If you still had $12M in assets at your passing, $1.5M would be subject to the estate tax. Gifting is one of the most straightforward strategies to minimize your estate. As I had mentioned earlier, the challenge here is that there are annual limits that may factor into your estate tax exemption over time.

One of the reasons gifting can be extremely advantageous is because often those gifted assets grow. For instance, if you were able to gift $15k in stock or real estate to a child today and that investment grew to be worth $50k in a few years, you may have just created a way to give much more in total while still staying within the annual gifting limits. If you were to wait until the stock grew, you would be over the $15k/year gifting limit when valued at $50k. This shows one of the most impactful strategies in estate planning, which is gifting to heirs or trusts early so those assets can accumulate in a way that is not considered part of your estate moving forward.

Here in Washington state, it is essential to note that, at this time, there is no lifetime gifting exclusion. This gives those with assets above the state level an opportunity to minimize their estate through large gifting strategies before passing, allowing them to keep under the threshold. Although this sounds like it may allow for freedom from this tax consideration, one of the challenges we often face is understanding our own mortality. We all feel inhuman until something comes up. Whether it's our physical health or our own mortality, we can't predict when terrible things may come up, making it difficult to rely 100% on this type of death bed gifting strategy. You may consider taking some measures ahead of time, even if between federal and state levels, to be sure that you may not leave your heirs with a massive tax bill after you pass.

A friend of mine had been working with an advisor at a big bank; let's just call them Big Bank Company for now. This family had done a great job of saving. They had a couple of rental properties and had managed to build a portfolio just shy of $3M in assets. All in total, with their rental properties, primary residence, retirement accounts, and life insurance, their estate was valued right around $7.5M.

I had brought up my concern about the estate taxes we experience here in Washington State. I shared the great opportunity we have to consider gifting assets right away to decrease their estate below the state estate tax level, given the gap between our state estate tax and the federal level, in case something were to happen. They were a young, healthy couple and the Big Bank Company advisor had given them the traditional advice, saying not to worry about it. She said this is no issue because if they get sick, they can simply give away their assets and not have any issues. On the surface, this seemed fair. I did my best to share my concerns and help them understand how quickly things can change.

Unfortunately, things did change. The couple passed away in an accident completely unexpectedly and with no time to plan. Because most of their assets were in IRAs and real estate, the kids were left with a significant estate tax bill and couldn't sell the real estate in time to handle the tax.

So, the kids had to take distributions from their parent's retirement accounts, paying income taxes on the distribution to pay for this estate tax bill. They were taxed twice! Some thoughtful planning ahead of time is all it would have taken to be sure to address this. The kids wouldn't have lost over half of the estate in taxes alone between the state estate tax and the income taxes on their assets.

Trusts

Outside of gifting, you can also use **trusts** to help get money out of your estate. One of the common misconceptions is that trusts are only for the ultra-wealthy. The truth is that trusts are not just for estate tax purposes. They can in fact be used for anyone who would like to establish more control and clarity at their passing.

The general idea behind a trust is to create an entity to distribute assets. This can also allow you to have much more control over how assets pass and help limit the probate process as much as possible, keep assets away from creditors, and keep records private. As we had discussed earlier, probate can be an extremely timely and painful process. If you would like to create a trust where all assets go into the trust and are distributed based on the parameters you set, you may be able to minimize probate significantly.

Trusts can also be used for those who have an estate tax concern, but not all trusts will help in this regard. However you use them, remember that when introducing legal concepts, there may be attorneys involved and certainly can incur costs to set up and maintain.

Revocable Trusts

There are two general types of trusts. The first is a revocable trust, and in this case, the name says it all! A **revocable trust** means that assets in this type of trust can be revoked, meaning you can take back control over your assets at any time. In more simple terms, you still have control over any monies put into this type of trust.

Those who would like to have more control of how their assets pass may use this type of trust to ensure their wishes are carried out, so their 18-year-old son doesn't spend the money on trips to Ibiza in the first year. You can get as detailed as you like with these measures. I even had a client once who was worried about making sure his children would still be contributing to society, and he set up measures to dictate the amount the kids were able to take out of the trust to match the amount they earned that year on their W-2. So, you can create a lot of control and specificity with a trust. If you still have control over an asset and discretion to do with them as you please, the IRS will consider this part of your estate. In this case, this type of trust would not help with those looking to get assets out of their estate to minimize estate tax implications.

Irrevocable Trusts

If you would like to establish a trust under the idea of tax planning, you may start exploring *irrevocable trusts*. Like a revocable trust, an irrevocable trust is simply an entity that allows all the same benefits around intentions, protection, and control. As you may gather from the name, the challenge is that irrevocable trusts are not as flexible as revocable trusts.

Generally speaking, when assets go into an irrevocable trust, you may not have access to these again. Irrevocable trusts are set up very specifically with rules and parameters that the trustee must follow when accumulating and distributing trust assets. However, because you give up this control, the asset is considered to be owned by the trust rather than an asset in your estate. This can help significantly with estate planning as a way to separate assets from your estate and still set up parameters so your heirs would receive your assets as you wish. Irrevocable trusts must pay separate taxes. They may also come with additional costs but will give great opportunities for effective estate planning if you find yourself in a position where you are concerned with estate taxes.

You can fund a trust with a number of assets. Typically, trusts are funded with liquid assets to help ensure there is some level of liquidity to pay for the trusts' taxes, expenses, etc., but they are not limited to this. Some folks may consider putting property or real estate into trusts. To leverage a death benefit, sometimes life insurance may even be used to fund trusts. This is where estate planning can get fun, and a bit more complicated. Estate planning is a big puzzle and figuring out the best fit for different pieces is the difference between a basic estate plan and the most efficient estate plan for your specific wishes.

Many of our clients have strong philanthropic intentions. Several of the strategies around gifting and trust strategies can work in the philanthropic arena as well. The purpose of this text is not necessarily to get into the ins and outs in this arena. Still, there are many nuanced strategies that those with philanthropic interests can use to both help in their tax and estate planning as well as make a large impact to the philanthropy of their choosing. While this area of financial planning is quite vast, if you do find yourself in this position, there are some great opportunities to explore.

Those with business interests may also need to understand how business equity may fit into the estate plan. Any ownership valuation is going to be included in your total estate. Such an inclusion can often pose issues. For example, if you own an interest in a small business, the value may not be very liquid, ownership issues can be very sensitive, and the impacts to the business may be huge if they go to the wrong person. In these scenarios, understanding the tax implications to your estate and developing strategies ahead of time to gift business interests or to create other liquid assets to pay for any taxes is critical.

Remember, as we discussed above, none of the exemption limits or strategies are permanent, but often the mechanisms can remain similar through time. Under the old model, we were told to put an estate plan in place once and let it go. Today, flexibility in your estate planning is key to be sure that you can adjust as legislation and policy changes. For instance, it may be helpful to take advantage while the estate exemption is high, in case it decreases in the future.

Effective estate planning is not just about the estate tax exemptions alone either, as many believe. Client estates may fall below this limit, but it's also important to understand our heir's tax implications with retirement accounts. This is another area the Roth can be a powerful tool. If you were to pass a traditional, pre-tax retirement account to your heirs, they would be forced to pay income taxes on their distributions as they are required to take that money out. If you pass a Roth IRA to your heirs, as it stands today in 2020, there would be no income tax implications to these distributions. Now, these assets would still be included in your estate, but you would be able to help them navigate income tax consequences of inheriting that asset.

Regardless of the complexity you find yourself in, the key to proper estate planning is understanding how your estate may be taxed, how assets pass, and what documents you may want to minimize the headache for your heirs. Even with the best intentions, it can be quite difficult to avoid the probate process altogether. However, the more thought you put into your estate planning today, the more you can streamline this process and make that probate process as minimal as it can possibly be.

Take it from someone who has dealt with this personally – and through many client stories – a family member's death, unfortunately, can bring the worst out in people. To minimize the arguing and make your intentions as clear as possible to your heirs, take the proper measures today to get your estate in order and help your family. Proper estate planning should involve a financial planner, an estate planning attorney, and a CPA, if needed, to be sure to address all angles.

X.   Conclusion

You made it! And if you took each of these chapters to heart, you should feel empowered to tackle your goals and build out a thoughtful plan.

Now that you have read through these categories go back through the text. Re-read the areas that you could brush up on and get a good grasp on these chapters in their entirety. You now have the tools and an understanding of the thought and personalized strategies it takes to really make the most of your resources. However, now you know exactly what to look for and the fundamental building blocks to help you build your ideal retirement in today's world.

This is intended to be an ongoing resource for all things finance, so please use this repeatedly. Now that you have the tools in your toolbox, you may need to go back to the shed occasionally to sharpen things up.

Please be cautious giving into the passive norm that retirement planning is as simple as saving X amount to set yourself up for a successful future. Something as crucial as financial freedom should not be a hands-off approach. It should take some work and intentional action. However, if you do the work and put in the thought, the future you will be thanking present you over and over again.

Unfortunately, we have been told some general rules of thumb our whole lives, and the more we hear it, the harder it can be to challenge this way of thinking. A child is born with a blank slate, but very quickly we start to establish beliefs. Some beliefs we have heard so many times that we don't even think to challenge them. If you want to really take charge of your finances, everything you need to know is right here in digestible bites. Running a marathon starts with the first step.

You may be "retired" longer than you work, and it is critical to understand that something this serious should take some thought to set up a life by design rather than happenstance. It may be possible to be comfortable with the typical retirement planning, but I implore you to consider if you would like to just "get by" in retirement or really set yourself up to live a life you dream of. Many of the folks who have taken the former route may seem good on the surface but may be just one medical challenge or unexpected shift away from disaster.

Use each of these chapters to focus on one area at a time if that makes developing your plan more manageable. These areas can be addressed one at a time but do not view them in silos. Every single change in one aspect will create a compounding effect in other areas. Understand the high level of these impacts and incorporate a cohesive plan across the board to really give yourself and your future self a leg up!

If you feel you could use some help, find a great financial planner that will be sure to look at all these areas with the level of detail they require. Whether building a strong team around you or working through this on your own, you now have the tools to take charge. Review your current plan today while everything is fresh. Ensure you are saving enough to hit your income goals, prepare for the unexpected, and address tax efficiency throughout your plan.

I will always remember a few of my first days of middle school. I was placed in an advanced math class, and my first day was far from easy. I will never forget my experience in my first day of this math class. Literally, the very first day, I was seeing equations that were utterly foreign to me.

I went home almost in tears, telling my parents I did not want to be in the class and that I wouldn't be able to do it. They forced me to stick with it for another week and see how that went. I ended up doing precisely that, mostly because they made me, but it was so good for me. I quickly picked up and caught up, passing through the year with a B.

Not only did this experience allow me to improve my math skills, but it also taught me a fundamental life lesson. I now live under the idea that I can actually do more than I think I can. If I force myself into uncomfortable situations and give it my all, I know I can grow exponentially. I realize this may be a lot of information and may feel overwhelming. But keep at it, keep reading this over and over where you feel stuck. Eventually, it will click, and you will be so happy you took the time or found someone to help create a retirement by design!

Now get started today! Don't let this fester and lose steam as the strategies you just learned become blurry. My biggest concern in writing this was that folks would read it but not act on a single item. Please don't fall into this trap of human nature and push off the action until tomorrow. You have the tools to create your ideal life, so get started today.

It may seem scary now, but the payoff is truly priceless. The norm is for people to read this, feel excited about a better future, but do nothing about it. So, let's break these norms and create a more thoughtful plan by taking one simple step today to get started. Start right away by taking your inventory, track down your assets and liabilities in their entirety, and find a place to enter this data to track it. It all starts with a strong foundation!

Once this is done you will notice a domino effect where you will become more and more motivated to build off this, slowly addressing each area we have discussed. After you have taken inventory, work on your Budget 2.0 that we had laid out in chapter three. Then, dig into the areas that are most relevant to you today. Keep coming back to this resource when you feel lost, and go forth, take control to build your retirement by design today!

Facebook:
https://facebook.com/MainsailFG

LinkedIn:
https://www.linkedin.com/in/blsteele

YouTube:
https://www.youtube.com/channel/UCLdYRyOCfH9XkfAJus3xNJQ
or search "Mainsail Financial Group"

Instagram:
https://instagram.com/theblsteele

Website:
https://www.mainsailfg.com

Glossary

4% Rule – A principal stating that retirees may be able to safely take a 4% distribution from their assets in retirement

401(k) – An employer sponsored retirement plan allowing you to save towards retirement

72(t) – Allows penalty free withdrawals from retirement accounts to those under age 59.5 as long as specific requirements are met

Asset Allocation – The specific amount we put into each asset class

Beneficiary – A named person or entity entitled to receive a benefit if you were to pass away

Bonds – An instrument of debt

Capital Gain – The amount of gain experienced in an investment outside of retirement accounts that would be subject to tax

Correlation – A measure of two investments similarities. A high correlation shows the investments move in lockstep, while a negative correlation shows they move in opposition

Credit Risk – The ability of an entity to pay back on their loans

Deflation – A measure that addresses a decrease in prices over a period of time

Diversification – The spreading of resources across different types of asset classes

ERISA – Employee Retirement Income Security Act of 1974 is a federal law that set minimum standards for most retirement and health plans

Estate Tax – A tax applied to a deceased individual's estate for assets above a certain threshold

Exchange Traded Fund (ETF) –A basket of stocks and bonds that trades instantly, similar to an individual stock

Full Retirement Age (FRA) – In reference to Social Security benefits, FRA refers to the age in which you will receive your full retirement benefit

Health Care Directive – A named person in charge of medically related decisions for you

Index Fund – An index fund follows a particular index and allows an investor to participate in that entire index performance

Inflation – The hidden risk that measures the increase in prices over a period of time

Investments – Putting money aside with the expectation of growth in the future, when investing we also introduce risk

IRA – A pre-tax retirement account that is owned by an individual which allows for tax deferral but will lead to taxable income in retirement

Irrevocable Trust – An entity created for estate planning purposes that allows the owner to establish a trustee. Assets put in an irrevocable trust may not be included in the owner's estate but are not revocable and the trustee dictates management based on the trust documents

ILIT – An irrevocable trust that owns life insurance for estate planning purposes

Interest Rate Risk – The risk of bond prices moving with interest rate fluctuations. As interest rates rise, bond prices decrease

Last Will and Testament – Estate planning document allowing you to specify who receives your belongings

Liquidity Risk – The inability to sell an asset quickly in the event of an emergency

Living Will – Estate planning document allowing you to dictate your "do not resuscitate orders" and how you may wish to be taken care of

Long Term Care (LTC) – Health services for those who are no longer able to care for themselves

Market Risk – The risk in a particular investment based on broader market events that impact the price of your investment without a direct relationship to the market event

Medicare – A federal program providing health care insurance for retirees

Medicaid – A state program providing long term care costs to those with low income and asset levels

Municipal Bond – A bond issued by a municipality to pay for public projects that provides income federally tax free but taxed at the state and local level

Mutual Fund – A basket of stocks and bonds that trades after the market closes each day

Net Unrealized Appreciation (NUA) - A complex tax planning strategy allowing those with company stock investments in their 401(k) to change the tax implications on this particular holding

Ordinary Income – A tax term referring to the way you would be taxed which would relate to the corresponding tax brackets at the time

Pension – A company sponsored retirement plan that provides a guaranteed income source

Power of Attorney – A named person to make decisions on your behalf

Probate – A state process of determining who and how your assets pass at your death

Rebalancing – The strategy of selling assets that have performed well and buying assets that have underperformed to stick to your ideal allocation

Revocable Trust – An entity created for estate planning purposes that allows the owner to revoke the terms but may not help with tax planning.

Risk – A broad term generally defining the trade off in order to provide hopes of investment returns

RMD (Required Minimum Distribution) – A required distribution on certain retirement accounts that force distributions every year starting at age 72

Roth IRA – An after-tax retirement account that is owned by an individual which allows for tax free growth and qualified distributions

Rule of 72 – A quick rule to determine how long it will take for your money double. You divide an expected rate of return into 72 to determine the doubling period (i.e. 72/6 = 12 years to double)

Savings – Money put aside with no expectations of growth but the instant ability to access

SECURE Act – Legislation passed in 2020 that changed the RMD rules on inherited retirement accounts, among many other provisions

Social Security – A federal program providing a suite of benefits to Americans who pay into the system during their working years

Step Up in Basis – Readjustment of the cost basis of a particular investment when passed to heirs

Stocks – An equity position in a company. If you own a share you will participate in that company's future whether up or down

Strategic Allocation – Refers to the long-term allocation strategy which is generally static

Tactical Allocation – Refers to the more nuanced changes in allocation that may be made periodically given market conditions, which is generally more dynamic

Tax Loss Harvesting – A tax strategy to sell assets at a loss to offset other gains in your portfolio

Trust – An entity established to transfer property to a beneficiary

Volatility – Measures the up and down movement in a particular investment